THE
PATTERNED
SHUFFLE
ATTACK:

A New Approach to Individual
Excellence and Balanced Team Play

THE PATTERNED SHUFFLE ATTACK:

ROBERT WACHS

A New Approach to Individual Excellence and Balanced Team Play

PARKER PUBLISHING COMPANY. INC.
WEST NYACK, NEW YORK

To my wife, Salona,
and my three boys,
Rich, Dave and Steve

©1974 *by*

Parker Publishing Company, Inc.
West Nyack, New York.

Library of Congress Cataloging in Publication Data

Wachs, Robert
 The patterned shuffle attack.

 1. Basketball--Offense. I. Title.
GV889.W32   796.32'32   73-17389
ISBN 0-13-654319-7

Printed in the United States of America

What This Book
Offers the Coach

Basketball's Patterned Shuffle Attack is a series of plays or options that continue until a shot is taken at the basket. If a shot is not taken or has not developed, then this series of plays is run once again. In other words, the Shuffle Attack is a pattern of continuity of play until a shot is taken. The only thing a coach can do is to develop his style of play by maneuvering his players into position to get a shot that is within his shot philosophy. An option or a play talked about above may be just one pass, just a dribble, or just a simple screen and a pass; but the development that the pattern gives is the continuity to go on to the next pass or screen if the preceding one did not work for the shot that the team is working for.

The book illustrates to the coach an offensive pattern that is adaptable to both a man-for-man and a zone attack. The emphasis is in *pattern*. This pattern is *movement* and *continuity*. When learning this movement and continuity, the player must control the pattern instead of the pattern controlling the player. Too many times, a shot or an opening will develop but the player does not recognize this opportunity and continues on with the play. This, then, is the pattern controlling the player. The player gets so engrossed with going into the next phase of the pattern that he fails to recognize the opening. When teaching the Patterned Shuffle Attack, the coach *must* avoid pattern control and not player control.

One of the advantages of this shuffle attack is that each player can be individually coached to use his greatest potential. To be an outstanding player, he should have the three basic basketball fundamentals developed—shoot, pass, and drive. A coaching point for the Patterned Shuffle is this—as coaches, we should be able to move the player, or players, into position where he gets an opportunity to use all three skills. The more individual excellence each player develops, the more balanced the team will be. Another Patterned Shuffle point is this—the more positions on the court where we can give the player a chance to operate and use his skills, the more balanced the attack will be. In this way, we should be able to move individual players into different parts of the court and not just in one part. The more positions they can work from, the harder they will be to defend. As shown in Chapter 4, the Patterned Shuffle Attack does give the coach the opportunity to move his players into various spots on the court.

Individual excellence can be used and developed by the player in his role as the driver or the feeder, as the weakside man as shown in Chapter 2, back to the original strong side man, as also shown in Chapter 2, and as the clear man as shown in Chapter 5. These are a few examples that the Patterned Shuffle Attack has used for the individual player which have developed fundamentals of passing, shooting, or driving.

Many good players need help freeing themselves just to receive the ball so they can use their basic skills. The double screen situation, as discussed in Chapters 2 and 3, is for these individual players. The split post situation, as discussed in Chapter 2, helps the player free himself by using the moving screen away from the pass by the point man.

The Patterned Shuffle Attack shows *three* basic tracks the shuffle cutter may take when walking his man into the post. Chapter 2 shows the front, back, and overhead pass option to the cutter. It will be shown and explained that the defense dictates to the cutter which track is to be taken each time this man runs his defensive man into the screen.

The Patterned Shuffle Attack is designed to place defensive pressure on the post's defensive man. Chapter 2 shows how the cutter helps free the post and how pressure applied by movement of the ball and the offensive man helps free him for what could be many inside board shots.

Any offense a coach uses should have a place for individual excellence at different positions on the court. This is what the

Patterned Shuffle Attack gives the Coach—excellence for the driver or excellence for the post man.

A ball club is not successful without a good sound defense. Chapter 10 gives the Coach some sound man-for-man defensive principles that are very adaptable to all levels of coaching. Chapter 12 gives the Coach a sound monster type of defense that can be used full, half, and quarter court. This monster type of defense combines man-for-man principles along with its zone trap ideas.

One of the very new type of offenses is the 1-4 set. Chapter 11 shows how the Patterned Shuffle Attack can be indoctrinated into, and used with, this 1-4 alignment.

Chapter 5 gives the Coach special situation plays that can be used with the basic shuffle offense. These clear outs, picks, and tracks are designed to look like the pattern and can be used as out-of-bounds plays or designed to be used in special situations such as after baskets or free throws. They can be designed to give players a chance to use their individual talents.

The Patterned Shuffle is a complete offense that uses the single post man for: scoring—feeding by splitting the post—screening for individual drivers or cutters—or uses him in the give-and-go situations. It gives an opportunity for individual play. If a coach wants movement and continuity in his offense, then the Patterned Shuffle Attack is designed to give the offense that comprises all of these situations.

The offensive movement, continuity, and defensive principles that will be discussed have been used successfully on both high school and college championship teams. I hope that this book, *The Patterned Shuffle Attack: A New Approach To Individual Excellence and Balanced Team Play*, will give the reader some basic ideas that will be useful to him.

Robert Wachs

Acknowledgments

In the basketball season of 1954-55, I had the privilege of being the assistant coach to Carter Burns, at Wyandotte High School, in Kansas City, Kansas. It was from Coach Burns that I received many ideas and it was he who advanced my knowledge of basketball and the shuffle offense.

I want to thank Coach Clark Swisher, athletic director at Northern State College, for the opportunity to coach at Northern. I also have to thank him for the time, effort, and guidance he has given to me these many years.

I know there will be many people outside the state of South Dakota who will read this book and the following names will have no meaning but to these players, and many more, I wish to thank for the many fond memories that they have given to me these past years.

Marv Rasmussen and Harry Marske started with me as freshmen in the fall of 1955. With the help of many others they went on to win four conference championships. That nucleus had a record of 89 wins and 18 losses—three of these losses were in the National N.A.I.A. Tournament in Kansas City.

Mel Klein (1957-61), NAIA-All American.

Jim Kampen (1959-62), NAIA Liston award winner in 1962.

Gary Nygaard (1960-63), DuWayne Groos (1962-65), Jim Schlekeway (1964-67). All three are members of the 1600 club or better.

Gary Evjen (1968-71), twice NAIA All-American.

I wish to acknowledge and thank Coach Pierre duCharme, Aberdeen High School Coach, for his time and help in developing the work with the 1-4 offense and the writing on the monster defense.

CONTENTS

What This Book Offers the Coach **5**

1. The Basic Series of the Patterned Shuffle Attack **15**

Formations • 16
Basic Working Formation (BWF) • 18

Hit the No. 1 Man in the Corner • 20
Hit the Post, No. 3 Man • 22
Hit the No. 4 Man • 24
Hit the Cutter (2 Man) • 27
Front Track • 28
Back Track • 29
Baseline Track • 29
Hit the No. 3 Man (Post) • 32
Drive by the WSW (No. 5) • 35
Continuity When the No. 5 Man Does Not Hit Anyone,
        Double Screen • 37
Reset by the WSW • 42
Back to the Original Strong Side • 43
Hit the Post • 46
Drive or Shoot • 48
Double Screen • 49
Reset • 52

Review • 53

2. Getting Into the Basic Working Formation **55**

Ten Series Entry Strong Side • 55

Ten Series, First Option of No. 1 Man • 57
Ten Series, Second Option of No. 1 Man • 59
Ten Series, Third Option, Hitting the No. 4 Man • 60

Getting Into the Basic Working Formation, (*Continued*)

Review of Ten Series, Strong Side • 64
Enter on Weak Side • 64

Bring the Ball Up the Weak Side, Ten Series • 65

Twenty Series • 69
Thirty Series • 71
Review of All Series • 73

3. Handling Trouble Spots with the Patterned Shuffle **75**

Situation (A), Interchanging • 75

The V Cut • 77
Guard Underneath • 81

Situation (B), Rotation • 83

Hitting the No. 2 Man on the Rotation • 85
Guard on to the Post • 86

Review Trouble Spots • 88

4. Using Special Plays out of the Basic Working Formation **91**

Strong Side Clear • 93
Interchange and Clear • 98
Rotation and Clear • 99
Overhead to the Post • 99
Baseline Pick for the Post • 103
Baseline Pick for the Corner • 105
Review Special Plays • 106
Special Clear Out from Pattern • 107

5. Setting Up a Zone Defense from the Patterned Shuffle Attack . . . **111**

Hit the Corner • 113
Hit the Post • 113
Hit the Point • 113

Weak Side Wing's Options • 115
Double Screen • 118

Setting Up a Zone Defense from the Patterned Shuffle Attack (*Continued*)

   Placement of Personnel • 121
   Back to the Original Strong Side • 123
   Cutter Sets Opposite the Post • 124
   Cutter Rebounder • 126
   Review Zone Offense • 126

6. **Coaching a Delay Offense from the Basic Working Formation 129**

   WSW Options • 129

      Hit WSW • 131
      Hit the SSW • 131
      Hit the SSW • 133

   Review the Control Game • 136

7. **Movement and Player Placement for the Patterned Shuffle 137**

   Tandem Left • 141
   Review • 142

8. **Drills for Teaching the Patterned Shuffle Attack 147**

   Double-Screen Shooting Drill • 150
   Weak-Side-Wing Shooting Drill • 151
   Lay-Up and Dribbling Drill • 152
   3-on-2 Fast-Break Drill • 153
   3-on-3 Drill, Full Court • 154
   One-on-One Defensive Drill, Full Court • 155

9. **Denying and Defense 157**

   The Ball Should Not be Dribbled between
         Two Defensive Players • 158
   Defense—Line of Flight • 161
   Defense and the Post • 162
   Defense and the Screen • 163
   Fast Break and Denial • 164
   Denial and the Shuffle • 166

Denying and Defense (*Continued*)

Other Denying Principles • 167
Review • 168
Trap–Denying–Defense • 169

10. 1-4 and the Shuffle 177

Twenty Series • 180
Use of Personnel • 180
Special Situations • 184
1-4 and the Zone • 186

11. Diamond and Monster Defense 189

Basic Perimeter • 190
The Diamond and the Trap • 199

Why the Diamond and the Monster: • 203

12. Zone Trap Offense 205

Index 211

The Basic Series of the Patterned Shuffle Attack

1

In preparing the Patterned Shuffle Offense, I have geared it to answer these questions: what will we do if the option and play do not work; where will my personnel be; how quickly can we reset; or can we just go into the next option of the continuity? The question of time will always enter into the coach's mind—"Am I spending too much time in learning movement and not enough time in teaching technique?"

It is wrong if a player has to think what he is going to do next, while the present play is running, because then he isn't giving his entire attention to the play that is being run. In football, a play is run, and if it doesn't work the team gets organized and can run the same play over again. It does get a chance to get itself organized without the pressure of the defensive team. Now in basketball, if a team runs a play and a shot is not taken, the team has to reorganize with the pressure of the defense. The less time and effort that this organization takes, the better off a team will be.

The basic movements of the Patterned Shuffle Attack will be explained in the following pages. Different movements have been used in some years and deleted in others. These various movements and options are given and the coach has to decide just which are the best movements for his club. Each club will change according to its personnel and each will run the same options differently.

It is impossible for any club to try to run all the movements and options that are given in the following pages. It would not be advisable to try to teach a complete new offense such as this all at once. A coach should decide on the best and basic movements to fit his club, and once these movements are learned, then more can be added. It is a fallacy for any coach to teach too much of a certain pattern or any type of offense until one part of it is well learned,

I will say this and repeat it, "That the pattern is of no value to a club if the pattern controls the players—the players must control the pattern." If the players have to think their movements through rather than react to the defense that causes the movements, then the pattern is going to hurt that player and the team.

FORMATIONS

The Basketball Patterned Shuffle Attack is run from two basic formations. These basic formations are called Tandem Right, Diagram 1, and Tandem Left, Diagram 2.

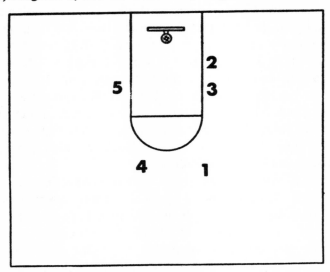

Diagram 1. Tandem Right, Formation 1.

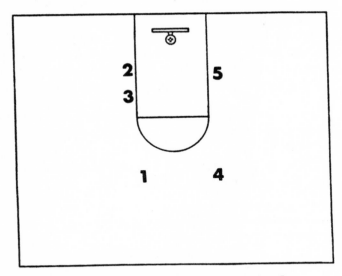

Diagram 2. Tandem Left, Formation 2.

We consider the right side to be the side of the court as the players are looking at their basket. The strong side of the court is determined where two men are set on one side. Usually, the strong side will be where the post and one forward are together. There could be situations when the so-called post will be on the weak side, which is where only one player is located, but he will still be numbered No. 5. As shown in Diagram 1, the right side is the strong side and the left is the weak side.

For convenience of following through in the pattern of play, we number the personnel. The numbers are explained below:

> No. 1—Strong-side guard.
> No. 2—Strong-side forward.
> No. 3—Post.
> No. 4—Weak-side guard.
> No. 5—Weak-side forward.

As mentioned, the weak side is the side opposite where two men set and the strong side is usually determined by a man who is called the post. It is imperative that each player knows which is the right or left side and which is the strong or weak side.

The normal position of the post, No. 3 man, is about three feet below the free throw line. This position will vary according to each coach, and it also varies with our club according to where the pressure is placed upon the guards bringing up the ball.

A general rule for the position of the weak side forward is just a shade lower than the post. The strong-side forward is behind the post.

In setting up our offense, I will use many diagrams and movements. The keys will be as follows:

– – – – – – – – – – –	Pass.
⟶	Movement of player.
～～～～～～	Dribble.
②	Player that has ball.

BASIC WORKING FORMATION (BWF)

To start our pattern of play and our basic movement we have to be in what I call our Basic Working Formation. This is shown below in Diagram 3.

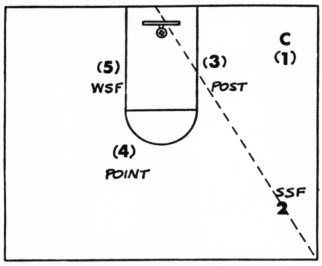

Diagram 3. Basic Working Formation, Right Side.

The SSF (strong-side forward) has the ball, post is about three feet from the free-throw lane, in the corner (c) is ready to receive a pass, and the point and WSF (weak-side forward) are ready to key their movements to what pass or dribble the SSF makes. Naturally, we set our BWF to the left side. (See Diagram 4.)

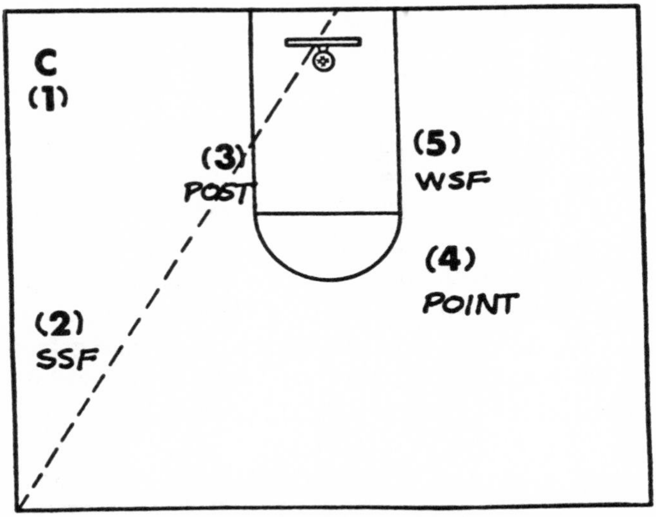

Diagram 4. BWF Left Side.

We can get into our Basic Working Formation in many different ways. If we have time to set up in our Tandem Formations, as shown in Diagrams 1 and 2, then we have three basic ways to get into our Basic Working Formations. These ways are designated as series:

1. Ten Series.
2. Twenty Series.
3. Thirty Series.

These three series and their movements to get into our Basic Working Formation will be discussed later in Chapter 3.

If, while coming down on the fast break, a shot does not develop, we have to try to scramble into our Basic Working Formation. The quicker a team can recognize that it is in its Basic Working Formation, the sooner its movement gets started.

The No. 2 man, the strong side forward, always has three

basic options once the Basic Working Formation is established. The Basic Working Formations, as shown in Diagrams 3 and 4, for the No. 2 are:

    1.   Hit the center.

    2.   Hit the corner.

    3.   Hit the point.

Hit the No. 1 Man in the Corner

If the ball is moved to the No. 1 man in the corner, the first thing the No. 1 man does after receiving the ball from No. 2 is to look at the post. If we hit the post, we naturally want him to shoot, but we can also crisscross the post from this floor position. When we hit the post from the corner we use this rule: The man to hit the post will go first. The No. 1 man goes and No. 2 tries to hook his man on the guard breaking from the corner. If the No. 1 man doesn't get the ball, he continues his screening and also blocks on the defensive man for No. 4. See Diagram 5.

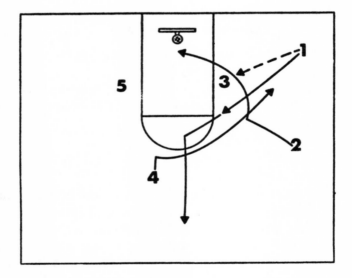

Diagram 5. Shows crisscross if the 1 man hits the center.

The shot by the No. 4 man is the hard option to stop if the screens are put on properly. The defensive man on No. 1 shifts off onto 2. This means 2's man takes 1; he then must shift again on to 4 if the screens are properly executed. As in all good screening, it is up to the man being screened for to set up his own defensive man. If the shot is taken by 2, we have 5, 3, and 2 rebounding. If 4 shoots over the screen, the 5, 2, and 3 still are in good position for rebounding. Any time we shoot we try to have men in good rebounding position. If a shot is not taken, we have to scramble into our Basic Working Formation. One way of doing this is to have No. 3 dribble to the forward spot and No. 5 come to the post position. (See Diagram 6.) We are now in our BWF and ready to run into our basic pattern.

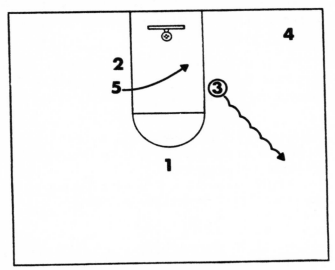

Diagram 6. Shows reset from corner split.

If we do not get the ball to the post from the corner, then the No. 1 man returns the ball to No. 2. Once again we are in our BWF.

The phrase, scramble back into our BWF, will be used many times throughout the chapter. There will be times when an option of the pattern will be used but no shot develops.

When this happens, the club has to get back into its Basic Working Formation to start the continuity of play all over. Once the BWF is established, the movement will start to try to get a shot at the basket. There will be times players can easily move into the proper spots but other times when it takes quite a bit of movement.

If all players know all spots, the BWF can very easily be established but if players have to be in certain spots then it takes more time and effort to get into our proper floor position. As mentioned earlier in the chapter, if when coming down on a fast break no shot develops, we have to scramble into our BWF. When doing this, we never will be in our Tandem Formations as shown in Diagrams 1 and 2. The post has to be established and the rest of the spots filled. In this manner we may set up quickly either on the left or right side.

Hit the Post, No. 3 Man

As No. 1 passes to 2, the post moves up and once again we are looking in at the post. When we are in our Basic Working Formation and the post is hit by No. 2, we have the following rules:

1. The baseline man, No. 1, breaks along the baseline looking for the pass. As a general rule, we like to clear the baseline and let the post man maneuver.
2. The SSF (No. 2) breaks over the top and screens for the No. 4 man. The post has the following options:
   a. Hit No. 1.
   b. Hit No. 4.
   c. Hit No. 5, who may be open because of a sagging defense man.
   d. Hit No. 2, who pops out at the point for defensive balance.
   e. As mentioned, we clear the baseline for the post who can operate to get his shot. We want the movement of the split to prevent the defensive men from sagging. Each post man will develop different types of moves and shots. (See Diagram 7 for the movement.)

This split is called our Strong-Side Split.

If no shot is taken by any of the above movement, we have to scramble into our Basic Working Formation. There is no set

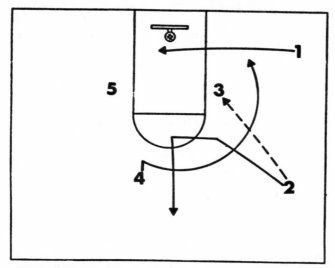

Diagram 7. Shows movement if post receives ball in BWF.

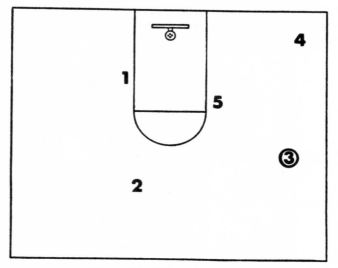

Diagram 8. Shows reset in BWF.

movement but once again No. 3 might dribble out to the 2 spot, 4 goes to the corner, 5 to the post, and 2 is on the 1 spot. (See Diagram 8.) We now are ready to go again into our basic pattern and movement from our Basic Working Formation.

Many times we will have trouble moving the ball from the corner to the No. 2 man, but we are prepared to handle this situation. This problem will be discussed later in Chapter 4 when rotation is described.

Hit the No. 4 Man

The third option of the forward is to move the ball to the No. 4 man. This is what we call going from the strong side to the weak side. As you recall, the strong side is determined by the position of the center. Sometimes, we will move the ball immediately from the strong side to the weak side, but other times, we will move the ball to the center or to the No. 1 man in the corner, then the progress of reversing the floor is delayed.

The forward sees the center is not open and then moves the ball to the 4 man. We want the timing to be such so that the No. 4 man will be hit when he is breaking for the ball. We also want him in the center of the court when receiving the pass from the forward. (See Diagram 9.) I want to stress at this time we do not want the No. 4 man in Position B. (Refer to Diagram

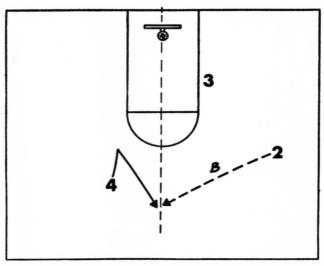

**Diagram 9. Position 4 should be in when receiving
pass from 2. Note: V cut by 4.**

9.) If No. 4 gets in Position B he will have trouble moving the ball to the wings. This then limits the options of 4. If, due to pressure, 4 does not get the ball at the point he must not come to the ball. What we do because of pressure will be discussed later in Chapter 4, in our section on trouble spots.

There are a number of things that have to be covered at this point. When 2 moves the ball to the point our names for some positions change. See Diagram 10. The reason for these name changes will be shown as we move on into our pattern of play.

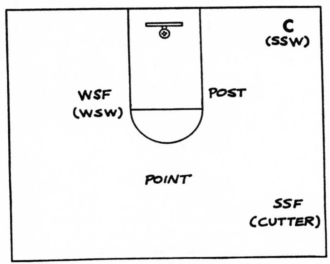

Diagram 10. C becomes SSW, SSF becomes cutter, WSF becomes WSW.

There are definite rules each player has to know at each spot and then react to them. At this time, I will give you the rules and then explain them as we progress.

1. If you are in the corner and the post is hit by a wing or a person drives at the post—clear the baseline.
2. If you are at the point and move the ball to a wing, then go away from the ball.
3. Any time you hit the post from a wing go over the top of the post and screen.

4. If you are the shuffle cutter and nothing develops, you reset opposite the ball or post.
5. When splitting the post—the shot is for the man on the point or the man coming to the point.
6. When the point has the ball he can move the ball to either wing.

As shown in Diagram 11 when 4 receives the ball there are three men that start to move. As mentioned in rule 6, the point

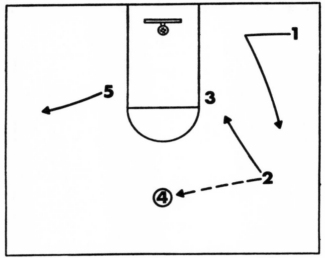

Diagram 11. Shows position of 4 when receiving ball from 2. Shows movement of 2, 1, and 5 when 4 receives ball.

can move the ball to either wing. A lot of pressure by the defense is put on our pass from 2 to 4 and from 4 (point) to 5 (WSW). Much time has to be spent on how to handle this pressure and later in the book these situations of pressure will be discussed. At this time I will assume that the point can move the ball to the 5 man (WSW).

The WSW should receive the ball to his outside. The No. 5 man should be about free-throw-line high and about two to three yards out from the free-throw line, as in Diagram 11. The first movement of 5 is to turn and face the basket. The options of the Weak-side wing when he turns and faces the basket other than just shooting are:

1. Hit the cutter.
2. Hit the post.
3. Drive.
4. Go into the double-screen situation.
5. Reset.

The following options are always available each time the No. 5 man receives the ball. Each ball player is different and will use his talents differently at this position. This is a good one-on-one situation and, depending on how well he drives or shoots, this really helps complement his passing options. As mentioned, each individual will operate and play this spot differently.

Hit the Cutter (2 Man)

An offense should have the threat of the lay-up. This is the one shot defensively we all try to prevent. The shuffle cut has been taught for years but it is still used by many coaches throughout the country.

As mentioned, many things happen at about the same time. At this time, I want to take the reader back to the No. 2 man when he passed the ball to the point. Remember, the No. 2 man is also now referred to as the cutter.

When the No. 2 passes the ball to No. 4, he should start preparing for his movement of trying to hook his man on the post, No. 3, man. His first move after passing to 4 should be to *turn* and *look* at his defensive man, take a step with his *baseline* (right) foot right at his man, and start taking him into his stationary screen, the No. 3 man. To make this cut successfully, many things have to be timed properly. The first part of the execution comes with No. 2 being in the proper position when he passes the ball to the point. I believe that the No. 2 man should be lined up in a straight line with the post and basket. (See Diagram 12.) How No. 2 gets into this position from our different series will be discussed in Chapter 3.

The cutter is taught three different tracks he may run each time he takes his man into the post. To a certain extent, the defensive man on the cutter dictates to him what track he will run. A coach can tell the offensive player what to do but he can't tell the defensive man what to do. So the offensive coach must teach the players how to run a certain track, depending on what a defensive man does in his defensing of the cutter. The three tracks the No. 2 man (cutter) can run are:

1. Front track.
2. Back track.
3. Baseline track.

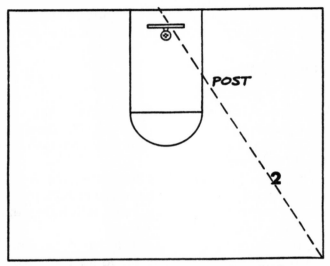

Diagram 12. Shows position for No. 2 on the floor.

Front Track

As mentioned earlier in this chapter, the cutter looks at his defensive man when walking him into the No. 3 man. If the defensive man is run into the post or goes to the baseline side to fight the screen we run the front track. (See Diagram 13.) Most teams will defense this man by having the defensive man going over the top of No. 3. If, by our movement, or if a defensive man does get careless and plays defense, as mentioned, then we want the above track run. This will not happen very often but when it does, a good pass from 5 gives the offense a good chance for a lay-up.

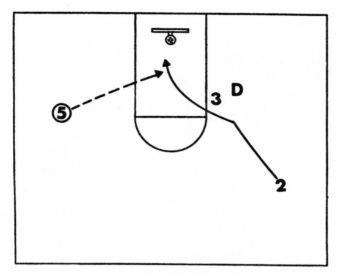

Diagram 13. Defense man on cutter goes baseline side.

Back Track

If the defensive man goes over the top as most defensive men are taught, then the cutter runs the Back Track. (See Diagram 14.) If the defensive man is slow recovering or gets tied up on No. 3's defensive man the cutter can be very open on the Back Track. The ideal spot to hit the cutter on the Back Track is just past the center of the court. (See Diagram 14.) Many times, the defensive man on the post will shut off this option and this can be expected. The proper track for No. 2 is to stop about a yard in front of the post, hesitate, then make a quick and timely break and try to get loose just behind the defensive post man.

Baseline Track

The third track is called our Baseline Track. As mentioned, I think the cutter should always make a short pause in front of the No. 3 man. This does give the No. 5 man a chance to turn and face the basket and as he is doing this his attention, many

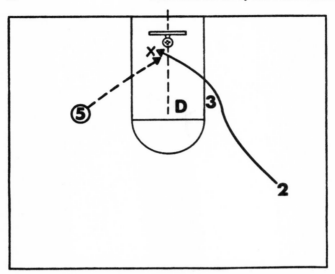

Diagram 14. Cutter takes Back Track.
X—ideal spot to hit cutter.

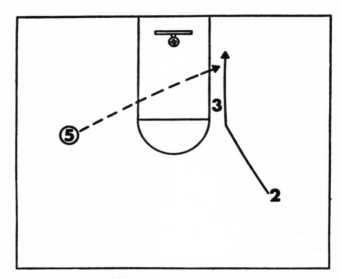

Diagram 15. Shows 2 man running Baseline Track

times, is right to the post and cutter. This pause does help the timing of the cut and also helps the WSW. Now the defensive man goes over the top, expecting to pick up the cutter as he comes off the Back Track, but instead of running this track, the cutter just slides down the lane and throws up his baseline hand as a target to the WSW. (See Diagram 15.) This third track has put added pressure on the defensive man on the cutter. Each defensive man will react differently on the three cuts. Some defensive men on the post will try to help the 2 man. We want the defensive post man trying to help out because this helps our post man to get free.

This Baseline Track has helped our Back Track because the defensive man on the cutter tends to stop about even with the offensive post. (See Diagram 16.)

If the defensive man stops as shown in Diagram 16, then a quick break, as explained in the Back Track, helps free the cutter for this track.

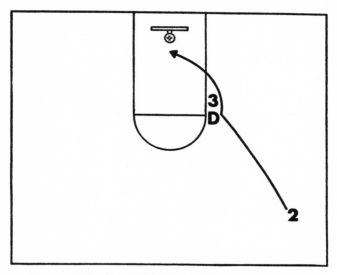

Diagram 16. Shows D of 2 stopping even with post.

Each time the cutter takes his man into the post he has three options available to him. Now the No. 5 man (WSW) does not know what track the cutter will take so it requires considerable timing to execute this play. As mentioned, the lay-up is the number one percentage shot in basketball and the coach has to decide whether or not it is worth all the effort and time to complete this perfect play. We expect each man on our squad to be able to run the WSW position and also the cutter spot. It takes time and patience on the part of the coach, and also the players, until they become proficient as the cutter and as a WSW.

Hit the No. 3 Man (Post)

The post man is the hub of our offense. As will be shown, the wings, the No. 2 man, and the corner are always looking at the post. This man has to feed cutters from the splits and work on his individual moves so he can score. The more proficient he becomes, the more valuable he becomes to the ball club.

It will be shown in Chapter 3 how and where the post is hit from the No. 2 on the Ten Series. The corner split has been discussed and also the strong-side forward split.

The better the post becomes, the tougher he is to defend so this then helps in freeing the shuffle cutter. We try to put extra burden on the post's defensive man by our movement of the ball, personnel, cutters, and because of the many spots from which we try to hit the post.

How and where the post man can be fed when the weak-side wing receives the ball will vary from game to game. One way of trying to help the post man free himself is help by the cutter. If the defensive post man likes to stay close to the post, we like to screen him with the cutter by taking the front track, regardless of what his defensive man does. (Diagram 17.)

This move is very effective if the defensive man becomes quite conscious of our baseline pass, which will be explained later in the chapter. Now the post might roll off and come low, he might come straight across, or he might come high across to free himself. This move will vary from game to game. It all depends on how each defensive man wants to try to defend the post man. Once again, I repeat, a coach can't tell the defensive man what to do so the offensive post man has to react and try to free himself with the different types of pressure.

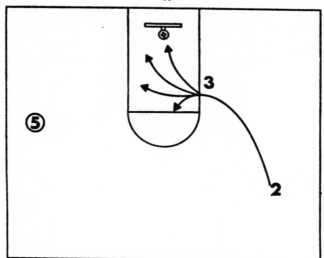

Diagram 17. Post comes right off of cutter's tail.
Note: 3 different tracks for post.

At times the defensive post man will play fairly high on the post and try to keep the cutter from coming across. (See Diagram 18.) The offensive post man should be aware of this high defensive position. We then would like to have the post man drop his baseline foot and roll to the basket. If the timing is right and the move executed properly, the post man will be free under the basket with the defensive man on his back. Some teams like to play this defensive man high to help jam our cutter. The post can make this offense roll on his own even before the cutter comes across. This is a hard move to see but the post man should know that it can be used and it becomes very effective.

The post man always comes across in some manner right after the cutter makes his break. If the cutter gets the ball, he is ready to rebound and if the cutter doesn't get the ball, the post works for position. If the post man doesn't get the ball inside the lane he continues to work for position along the free-throw lane. (See Diagram 19.) If the post is hit by the WSW in this position, we then, again, split the post. This is called our Weak-Side Split. We should be approximately in the following positions at this time. (See Diagram 20.) The explanation for the approximate position of the players is given in the rules listed on pages 25 and 26.

Note: Arrows show movement as 5 has the ball.

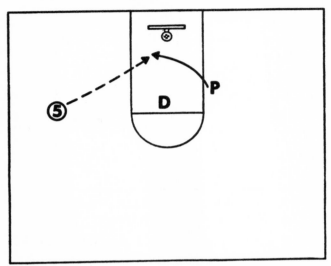

Diagram 18. Shows defense post man playing high.

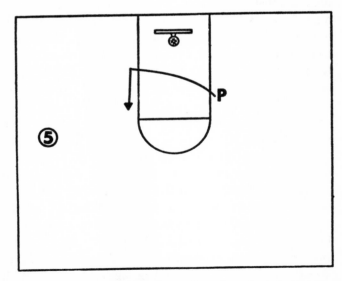

Diagram 19. Shows post working along free throw lane.

1. Cutter—if you don't receive the ball set opposite the post.
2. Point—After moving the ball to a wing go away from the ball.
3. Corner has moved from strong side wing to position as shown. Now the post is hit as he moves up the lane. (See Diagram 21.)

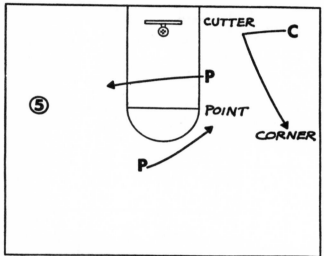

Diagram 20. Shows approximate position of all 5 men when post comes across.

Rule: WSW goes over the top to block for the man who is coming to the point, who is the corner man, SSW. We also block on the corner's defensive man by the point who goes away from the ball when he moved the ball to No. 5 (WSW). As in all our splits, the baseline is free for the post to operate for his shot or he can pass off. If no shot is taken the team has to scramble into their Basic Working Formation. (Diagram 22.) As mentioned, we have to try to scramble back. The ball could be moved out to WSW, who is our back man. He could dribble over to the No. 2 spot, SSW goes once again to corner, point comes out, and we now are in our Basic Working Formation on the left side and we start our movement all over looking for a shot.

Drive by the WSW (No. 5)

Any time the No. 5 man receives the ball, he has the option to drive the ball. *Example:* The 5 man receives the ball

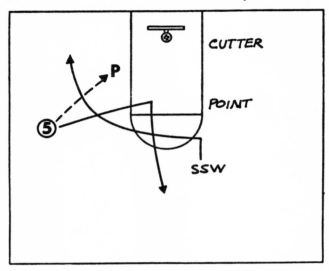

Diagram 21. Movement from WSW Split.

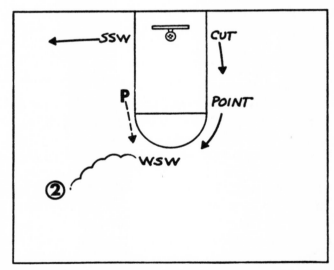

Diagram 22. Shows one way to scramble back to the BWF.

from the point and turns to face the basket as though to shoot. As the defensive man comes up, we then hope the WSW can take advantage of this latter move and drive the baseline.

The 5 man looks in on the cutter but he is covered. He might then drive hard at the free-throw lane for the shot or he might reverse pivot and try to pick his man on the post. This gives the good dribbler a real opportunity to play one-on-one or to use the post to free himself.

The WSW looks in and tries to find the post. If the post is covered, the WSW drives at the free-throw line. If a wing drives, we try to have the same basic movement if the Post is hit by the No. 5 man. (See Diagram 23.) What shot develops off the movement we cannot anticipate: 5 may shoot, hand off to the SSW coming to the point, or he may drive all the way to the basket. This is not a controlled situation and each driving by the WSW will develop its own opportunity. If no shot is taken, we just have to scramble back into our BWF and try for one.

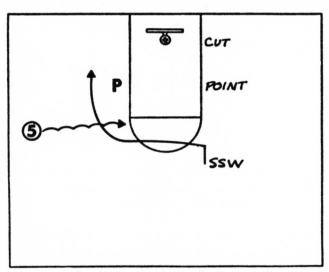

Diagram 23. Movement when WSW drives.

Continuity When the No. 5 Man Does Not Hit Anyone, Double Screen

If the No. 5 man does not hit either No. 2 or No. 3, or doesn't drive, we then have men in the following position. (See Diagram 24.) We now are ready to go back again to the right side, which has become the weak side. Note position of 2. As mentioned in rules that were given, the cutter will position himself opposite the post if no shot has developed for him. The rule for the point is to go away from the wing that he has passed to. As 4 is going away from the point position, the wing opposite the ball, who is the No. 1 man, SSW, starts to come to the point spot. Another way of putting this is—the point and SSW are moving while the WSW runs out his options.

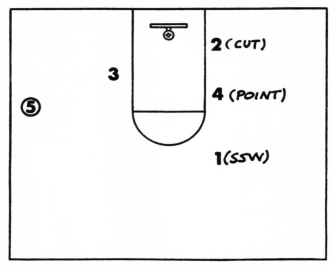

**Diagram 24. Shows all men in approximate position
if 5 didn't hit any options.**

If nothing develops, the SSW breaks for the ball. His first option is to turn and square off with the basket and shoot. (See Diagram 25.) Diagram 25 shows where all five men are when the SSW, No. 1, receives the ball. As soon as No. 5 hits 1, he turns and starts walking his man into the post. If 1 shoots, 5, 3, and 2 are in good rebounding position. If 1 does not shoot, the No. 4 man, point, breaks straight up the lane; he is getting into position to receive the pass from No. 1. Diagram 26 shows position and movement as No. 1 passed to No. 4. As shown, there is a lot of movement as No. 4 receives the ball. As mentioned, the WSW started to walk his man into the post, and

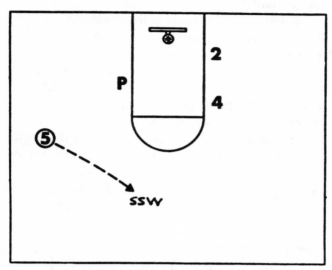

Diagram 25. Shows position of all five men
when 1 receives the ball.

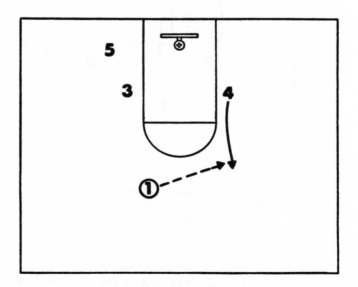

Diagram 26. Shows movement of men
after 1 has moved ball to 4.

No. 1 goes inside the lane to rebound and block on the WSW's defensive man. This block will be made if the defensive man on 5 comes up the lane. As No. 4 is squaring himself with the basket, No. 2 comes up and blocks on No. 4's defensive man. Now, No. 4 has the options of shooting, driving, or passing to No. 5 who is coming in front of the Post. (See Diagram 27.) The shot for No. 5 will usually be in front of the post man. If he receives the ball and his man has fought through the screens by 3 and 1, he might try to drive back to the baseline for the shot. The No. 5 man will make his play according to how the defensive man tries to play him. We have found out that the defensive man usually will come up the lane side behind the post and he will be picked by the No. 1 man going straight down the lane.

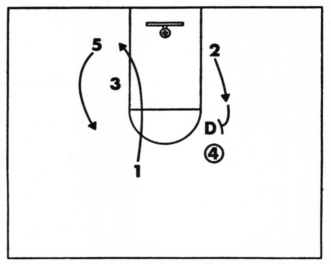

**Diagram 27. Shows movement (approximate)
as No. 4 squares off to the basket.**

The back track option is occasionally open. The defensive man tries to come up the outside of the post to keep No. 5 from getting the ball. The better the shooter, the tougher the defensive man will play. The WSW tries the back track for the pass. (See Diagram 28.) If no shots develop from the double-screen situation then we have to scramble back into our Basic

Working Formation or just reset. Diagram 29 shows the
approximate positions of all five men if no shot develops from

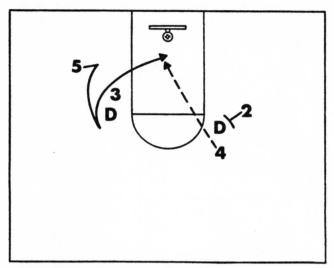

Diagram 28. Back track on Double Screen.
Defensive man tries to come outside of post.

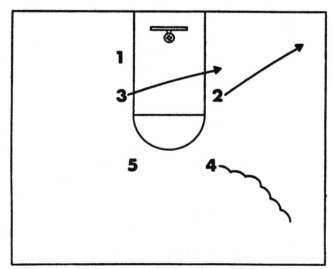

Diagram 29. Approximate position of all five men
if double screen didn't work. Shows
movement to scramble into BWF.

the double screen. If 4 had the ball, he could dribble over to the 2 spot, post moves into position, 2 moves to the corner, 5 becomes the point, and the 1 becomes the WSF. We are now in our BWF, each man would assume the numbers of his new position, and we are all set to go into our pattern of play as previously discussed.

Reset by the WSW

If the WSW does not hit the cutter, the post, does not drive, or go into the double-screen situation then the final option for the No. 5 man is to reset. We should be in the positions as shown in Diagram 30. Now the WSW just has to

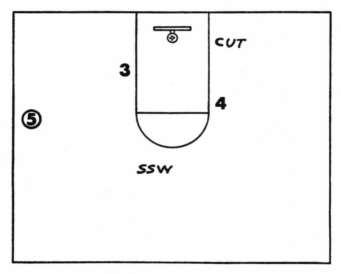

**Diagram 30. Position of all five men
if WSW doesn't hit any options.**

take a short dribble back, the No. 1 man goes to the corner and we are in our Basic Working Formation on the left side. Now the WSW is our No. 2 man, the 2 in this case becomes the No. 5 man. This very easily shows why each man has to be able to run all spots.

I would like to stress again at this point the floor position of the No. 2 man. As shown in Diagram 12, the No. 2 man should be in a straight line with the post and the basket. When the WSW receives the ball, he should be free-throw-circle high and when he dribbles to reset he should dribble up and not just out. The cutter can run a much better track from this position than if he starts his track even with the free throw line.

After the reset dribble the men should be in position as shown in Diagram 31. Now the WSW, who has become No. 2, has the same three options as the No. 2 on the right side in our BWF:

    1.   Hit the post.
    2.   Hit the corner.
    3.   Move the ball to the point.

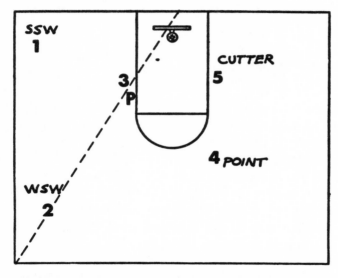

Diagram 31. Shows position of men after reset dribble.

Back to the Original Strong Side

Any time the Point, No. 4 man, receives the ball from the SSF, No. 2 man (see Diagram 9), he has the options to move the ball to either wing, weak-side wing or strong-side wing.

Sometimes the defense will not let the team enter to the WSW so the point will move the ball to the SSW. Then there are times we definitely want to move the ball to just the SSW.

Just as a review, when the point receives the ball we are in position to start the movement as shown in Diagram 11. Diagram 11 shows the movement of the SSF, who has become known as the cutter, corner becomes the strong-side-wing, and the WSF becomes weak-side-wing. The strong-side wing will not get into position to receive the ball as quickly as the WSW, due to the distance and type of track that he must run. The point moves the basketball to the SSW because of pressure or because he has been told to come back to the original strong side. Later, I will discuss why he should come back.

The strong-side wing should receive the ball approximately free-throw-circle high. He now has the following options:

1. Hit the post.
2. Drive or shoot.
3. Double screen.
4. Reset.

Before discussing each option there are a few things to mention. The rule has been stated that the point goes away from the ball or the wing that has been hit. Now this is true when he hits the SSW. We want this man moving when the wing is handling the ball. (See Diagram 32.) As he goes away from the ball, he looks for the WSW's defensive man and tries to force him to the inside. When the weak-side wing does not receive the ball and he sees it moved to the SSW, he starts his movement in and comes to the point. See Diagram 32 for his movement.

The cutter does not know if the WSW has been hit until he looks up for the ball. His attention is concentrated on walking his man into the screen. If the ball is passed to the SSW then his rule is to set opposite the post. This rule prevails on all three of his tracks. (See Diagram 33 on his reset position.) Naturally, he will be in different spots when the SSW receives the ball but he then readjusts his position and goes as shown in Diagram 33.

If it isn't predetermined to come back to the original strong side, the post, at times, will make his move with the

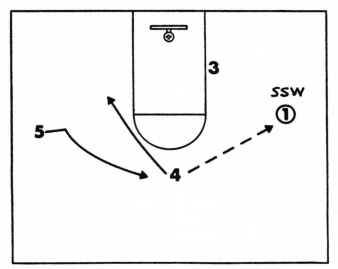

Diagram 32. Shows movement when SSW receives the ball.

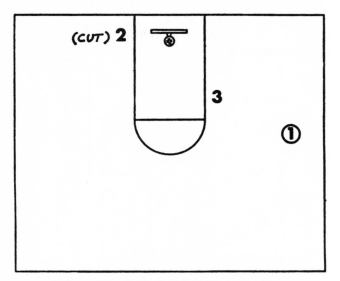

Diagram 33. Shows reset position of cutter.

cutter. He then has to reset his position back on the post. When the point receives the ball, his attention is divided on the ball, his man, and the defensive man on the cutter. He has to be aware of all these things so he might lose the ball before it comes back to the SSW. If he has made his move to go to the weak side for a pass, he just has to make it back to the strong side.

Hit the Post

The post man has a lot of activity around him each time the ball is passed to the point. As mentioned, his concentration is on the ball, his defensive man, and the cutter's defensive man; but his activity is also around the defensive man on the post. How each team will handle the shuffle cutter and how each team will play defense on the post will vary with each club that we play. Our philosophy is to put a lot of pressure on the post's defensive man. What he will do when the point receives the ball will vary with each club, the time situation on the clock, and naturally the threat of the offensive post. When the point receives the ball the defensive post man doesn't know where the point will move it. The first option of the SSW when receiving the ball from the point is to look at the post and try to hit him with a baseline pass. (See Diagram 34.) When the SSW receives

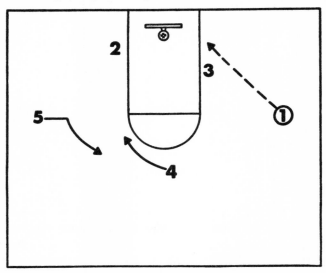

Diagram 34. Baseline pass by the SSW.

the ball, the position of the cutter will vary according to the track he has taken but he will reset opposite the post as shown in Diagram 33. As mentioned, the post does not know what his defensive man does when the point has the ball, but he should work hard to learn to drop the baseline foot and try to hook his man and be ready for the baseline pass. If the option is successful, the post has a good opportunity to score. If the post does not succeed in hooking his man as he slides down the baseline he works himself up toward the ball and once again he can be fed the ball. If he is hit in the position, we split. The rule for the SSW is to go over the top and screen. The point already has tried to force the defensive man on the WSW in so the SSW also blocks on the WSW's man. The post now has the options of hitting the WSW, point, SSW who pops out, or the cutter underneath on the opposite side. (See Diagram 35.)

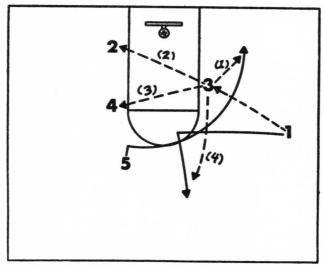

Diagram 35. Shows movement and passing options of post on SSW split.

As in most of our splits, the baseline is cleared and the post has the option of working to get himself free for a shot or hitting any of the men as mentioned. What options are open will vary with each split. If no shot is taken, the man with the ball takes a dribble and the team has to scramble into its Basic Working Formation. *Example:* The post moves the ball out to SSW who in turn dribbles to the 2 spot, WSW to corner, post stays set, point and cutter are in position. (See Diagram 36.)

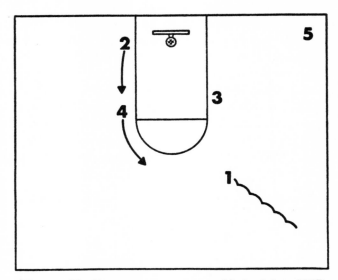

Diagram 36. Shows one way to scramble back into BWF.

Drive or Shoot

When the ball is moved back to the SSW, the floor is cleared for just the two men, post and SSW. What options or opportunity the SSW wants to use will vary according to each individual who is placed into this position. Some players are good shooters, others are drivers, some are both. Many different options prevail at this position. The SSW might break into this position and come right up with the shot. If he shoots, the post, cutter, and point are all in good position to rebound. Perhaps the SSW wants to drive the baseline or toward the middle. When a wing drives, we try to have basically the same movement as when the post was hit and we split; but now the wing controls the play instead of the post. What this drive develops will depend upon how a defensive man plays this wing. Naturally, this will vary from game to game and man to man. If he drives the baseline and no shot develops, the WSW comes over for the release.

If the wing drives to the top of the post as shown in Diagram 37, then many free lance options develop:

1. Stop and shoot.
2. Reverse pivot on the post, go back to the baseline, shoot, or if a shift develops, hit the post.
3. Hand off to the WSW.
4. Drive down the middle—if a shift develops by the post, hit him; if a shift develops by the cutter, hit him.

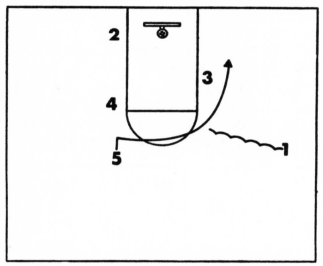

Diagram 37. SSW drives to the top of the post.

It seems the middle is really jammed but many of the men are moving into position as shown in Diagram 32, so that means the defense men are also moving. Once again, if no shots develop from this movement, the ball has to be moved out and the team has to scramble back into the BWF.

Double Screen

The Double Screen option for the SSW works just the same as it does for the WSW. If the SSW does not hit the post, and does not drive or shoot, then we are moving into our next phase of the continuity of our pattern. If neither one of the options above worked, we should be approximately in the following spots as shown in Diagram 38. Now the WSW comes to the ball and should receive it even with the free-throw lane boundary line extended. The SSW now starts walking his man toward the baseline. As he is doing this, the WSW turns and looks for the shot. (See Diagram 39 for the movement.) If the WSW shoots, the SSW, cutter, and post are all in good rebounding position. If the WSW does not shoot, the point breaks straight out to receive the ball. He now controls the play. He may:

1. 'Shoot.
2. Hit the SSW breaking out or under.
3. Drive using the cutter for a pick.

See Diagram 40 for position as Point receives the ball. What options develop for the point will vary in each situation when this man has the ball. It will vary for each individual as to who receives the ball in this position. No one knows what will

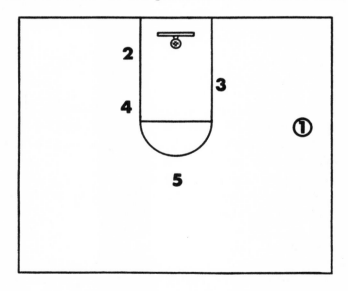

**Diagram 38. Shows approximate position of all
5 men if SSW didn't hit post or drive.**

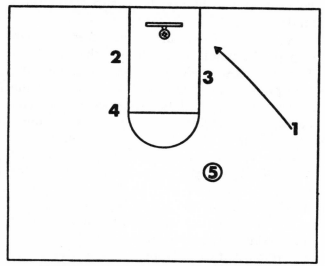

Diagram 39. Shows movement of SSW as WSW faces the basket.

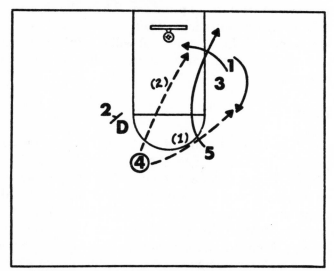

Diagram 40. Movement when point receives ball.

develop but the better the shooter and driver each man is in this situation, the more things can develop. Note the cutter's position on the defensive man on the point and note the WSW blocks inside the post. As he blocks, he is also getting into position to rebound.

The man to get the shot from our double-screen situation is the man coming to the point. You will note that this is an opposite wing. In our weak-side wing's option it was the SSW, and in our SSW's option it was the WSW. As mentioned the point, as he goes away from the ball, blocks on the wing's man. This forces the defensive man inside and if this wing then comes hard to the ball he gets a lot of shots from this movement. If this man is not open as he gets the ball, then he moves the ball to the point. The WSW goes straight down the lane to block for the SSW. We do not want him to stop to block or go to the outside of the post to screen. If the screen is placed properly, then the SSW has a good percentage shot in front of the post or he can drive to the baseline for his shot. If no shots develop, the point has to take a dribble and we scramble into our BWF.

Both double-screen situations for the SSW and WSW are identical in execution and movement. All players must be able to run and operate all positions. Where the shot develops in our double-screen situations again varies each time the double screen occurs. Each individual will run this situation differently and this in itself makes it interesting to use and tough to defend.

Reset

The fourth option of the SSW is to reset the ball club. The position that the players should be in is shown in Diagram 41. The SSW now takes a dribble out to the 2 spot, the WSW goes to corner, post is in his position, and the point and cutter just move up. The team is now in our Basic Working Formation on the right side and they are once again ready to start the pattern of play from the right. *Example:* The ball then could be moved to the point, who now once again controls our play. The SSW is now the cutter, the cutter becomes WSW, and the WSW becomes SSW. As mentioned, the point could move the ball to either wing and what develops then depends upon which wing receives the ball.

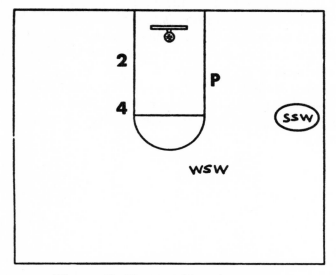

**Diagram 41. Shows position of players
if SSW doesn't hit any options.**

REVIEW

This is a good spot to review a number of things that have been discussed. The reader should note at this time how similar the two wings, WSW-SSW, are in the execution of their options:

WSW	SSW
1. Hit the cutter and post.	1. Hit the post.

Note: No cutter option for SSW, but post can be hit and split. The post is hit differently but the split movement is quite the same.

2. Drive at post or baseline.	2. Drive at post or baseline.
3. Double screen.	3. Double screen.
4. Reset.	4. Reset.

A coach can delete any of the options of the wings. If he doesn't want to teach the double-screen option, he just deletes this option from the wings. That just gives him one less option to work from. In some games, the drive at the post never comes up or the double-screen option is never run. We split the post from both wing spots but the movement is to help free the post so a team can't sag on the post. Naturally, the splits could very easily be deleted.

The reset from both wings is a very important option. This option gives the team a chance to regroup, gives it continuity, and also gives the team an opportunity to control the basketball.

Getting Into the Basic Working Formation

2

We use three series to get into our Basic Working Formation (BWF): Ten Series, Twenty Series, and Thirty Series. The time for any series to be run may be designated before the game starts. *Example:* On baskets made, we will run the Twenty Series; or on free throws made or missed by the other team, we will run the Twenty Series. There are numerous ways this movement can be designated.

One of the main reasons for the different series is the placement of personnel. There will be times when pressuring by the defense will not allow a club to place the personnel and then a club has to make its adjustment. Each series will place the offense players in different spots and this creates defensive problems, but the basic pattern from each series is the same. Due to placement of personnel and from its basic movement, one series might be more applicable in one game than another. It is not imperative that a team use all three series but the more different looks a team can give a defense, the more and better maneuverability this team will have in each game.

TEN SERIES ENTRY STRONG SIDE

We will start our basic pattern from one of the two formations as mentioned in Diagrams 1 and 2. Unless for some specific play or situation, no one knows what formation is being set up each time down the court. A coach can very easily say always set up in Tandem Right or Tandem Left. We usually will have our big man designated as the No. 3 man, who is the post man. As a general rule, we do not designate a certain man in any other designated spot. To simplify teaching to start the pattern, a coach can designate each player to be in a specific spot. In other words, for convenience of coaching, a coach can say that we will only use Tandem Left Formation and each player will always be in the same position each time down the court. Our general philosophy will usually designate the post man and then the rest of the players assume and execute the movement of that position as the players go into the continuity of play. In other words, one time down the court the guard will be the No. 1 man and the next time he might be the No. 4 man. This same thing applies to the two forwards. No one knows what will be the weak side or strong side unless this has been designated.

No matter where the pressure is applied, it is up to our guards to get the ball up the floor and into the playing area.

If we are being pressured full court, we generally will use the clear out method of bringing the ball up the court. We work and try for the guard bringing the ball up the court to try and keep the ball around the middle of the court and in this way we can enter in the strong side or weak side. The guard without the ball leads the dribble and tries to keep opposite the ball. (See Diagram 42.)

First: No. 1 has to work himself free to get the ball. There might be times when we have to bring another man down to help free the guard and then clear out all personnel. A coaching point is for the No. 1 man to face his man when receiving the ball and let No. 4 clear out. No. 1 should not use up the dribble as soon as he receives the ball. When the No. 1 guard works his way up the court, the No. 4 guard should be ahead of him but opposite him on the court. *Example* (shown in Diagram 42): If No. 1 is approximately at A spot, No. 4 should be at B as 1 works to C spot, 4 works to D spot. When No. 1 enters into the front court, he is ready to enter into our pattern of play.

It will be shown that before entry into the Basic Working Formation from our Ten Series there will be some movement and activity before the BWF is established.

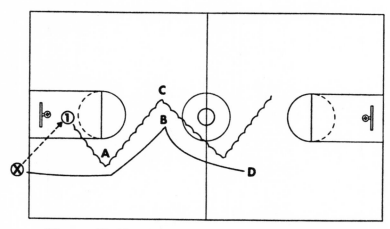

Diagram 42. Movement of guards when pressured full court.

First we will consider our pattern when bringing the ball up the strong side of the court. We will assume that the right side is to be the strong side of the court. The strong-side guard, No. 1 man, has three options each time he brings the ball up the court. These options are:

1. Hit the No. 2 man.
2. Hit the center, No. 3 man.
3. Hit the other guard, No. 4 man.

There is no sequence as to the order of hitting any of the above options, but certain pressure or over-playing by the defense will force some options or take away others.

Ten Series, First Option of No. 1 Man

When the No. 1 man is being pressured and is ready to move the ball to No. 2 breaking out, the players should be in position as shown in Diagram 43. This diagram shows the approximate position of players, with the right side the strong side. When receiving the ball, the No. 2 man should be higher on the court than the post and one to two yards from the side line, the No. 3 man about one yard below the free throw line, No. 4 about even with the No. 1 man, and the No. 5 just below the post.

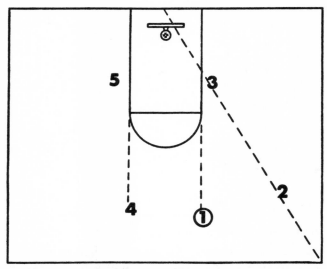

**Diagram 43. Position of players when No. 1 is ready
to move ball to No. 2 on the right side.**

The main option of putting the ball into play by the guard is hitting the No. 2 man coming out to meet the ball. The No. 1 man now goes to the corner. This then puts us in our Basic Working Formation. (See Diagram 44.)

As the No. 1 man moves to the corner, the No. 2 man, after receiving the ball, is to turn and look at the center. Occasionally, before our BWF is established from our Ten Series, pressuring causes a defensive man to be caught in B position as shown in Diagram 44. We would like to have the post man put up his inside hand (left in this case) as a target for the SSF. If the defensive man is slow recovering, and the pass is made properly, the post man should get the ball inside for a good opportunity to score. The pass to the post to the inside must be made before the No. 1 man gets to the corner. The pass will not be made many times during a game but when it does open, it gives the post an excellent opportunity to score.

As we mention movements and options it can be seen that many things are happening about the same time. The movement of the No. 1 man is happening at about the same time the No. 2

man is turning and looking at the basket and center. Once No. 1 moves to the corner, our BWF is established.

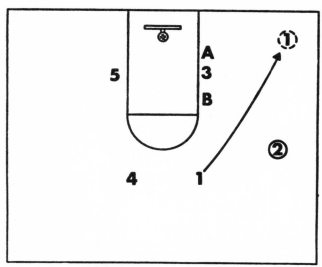

**Diagram 44. Movement of No. 1 when he hits 2. Shows
two different positions of defense on No. 3.**

Ten Series, Second Option of No. 1 Man

A second option of the No. 1 man in the Ten Series, when bringing the ball up the court, is to hit the No. 3 man. If the defensive man is pressuring the pass to No. 2, then we can try to move the ball directly to the post. The post should see that the No. 2 man is being pressured and should try to move up toward the ball and receive a pass from the No. 1 man. If the pass is made to the 3 man, the 2 man should break to the basket. (See Diagram 45.) If the play is executed properly, a lay-up may be had by the No. 2 man. After making the pass, No. 1 moves and screens for No. 4 who becomes the second option for No. 3. As shown in Diagram 45, No. 1 continues down and 5 comes out for defensive balance and also as a release for No. 3. If no shot is taken, we have to scramble back into our Basic Working Formation. This is a tough option to execute but occasionally, due to pressure, a back door lay-up can develop.

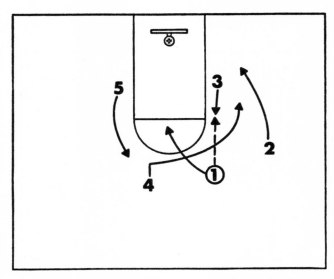

Diagram 45. Shows movement if 3 is hit by 1.

Ten Series, Third Option, Hitting the No. 4 Man

A third option of the No. 1 man in the Ten Series, when bringing the ball up the court, is to hit the No. 4 man who is the other guard. (See Diagram 46.) The biggest danger of this pass is an interception by the defensive man on No. 4. The basic idea of our play by our three options is to make the defensive players play it honest. The guard makes his fake to the No. 2 man and then passes to the No. 4 man. I would like to state that the No. 2 and No. 3 men might be so covered that the ball can't be moved to them. If the No. 4's defensive man sags on the center, then we don't have any trouble with the pass; but if he is pressuring No. 4, we feel that we should be able to hit the post by the No. 1 man. I want to stress again at this time that it is up to the guard to run the options where the defensive men are not playing. As a general rule, no one knows what option we are going to run so the guard controls the pattern of play. It is the responsibility of each player to be ready for any of the options. We will use the option of hitting the No. 2 man and No. 3 man most but it is up to the guards to vary our pattern of

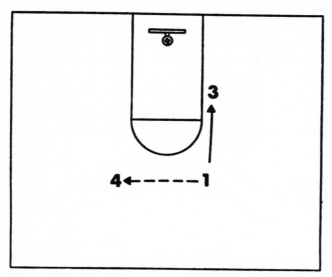

Diagram 46. Shows track of 1 after passing to 4.

play. At this point, I would like to take the play of each individual. All of these moves will be happening about the same time.

After the No. 1 makes his pass to No. 4, he moves straight down the free-throw lane, looking for No. 2's defensive man so that he can get a moving screen for him. He continues down the lane and gets into rebounding position. (See Diagram 46 for 1's movement.) In this way, 3 and 1 are setting a double screen for 2. (See Diagram 47 for 2's track.) As 2 comes out and sees the ball moved to 4, he automatically turns, faces his defensive man, takes a step with his baseline foot toward his man, and he is now in the proper position to take his man into the double screen set by 1 and 3. He tries to run his man primarily into the post. Usually in this situation, the pass will be from the 4 man but it may be from the opposite forward if 4 moved the ball to 5. The 5 man breaks into his weak-side position as he sees the ball moved to 4. Here, we usually want the 4 man to fake a pass to the 5 man and he then should feed the No. 2 man coming off the double screen. If 5 draws his man out when the 2 man receives the pass, he is in the position for a lay-up if a good pick was made by 1 and 3. A coaching point I would like to stress here is that the 2 man should try to pick up the 1 man, who is practically leading interference for him down the lane. This is a good option when the defense is continually trying to press the 5 man when the ball is moved to 4. This leaves the lane fairly well open for the 2 man. This is why a good fake has to be made by 4 to 5 so that 5's man will be drawn out of the lane.

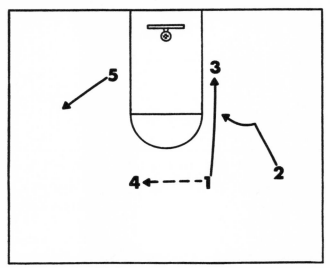

Diagram 47. Shows track of 1, 2, 5
after 1 passes to 4.

There are a lot of men moving at the same time and around the same spot but we have at times been successful in getting a good left-handed lay-up shot at the basket. A move that can be made from the above option is this: The defensive man on 1 will try to overplay his man and will not let the guard move the ball to the 2 man. Now to keep him honest, a quick pass to 4, and instead of 1 looking for and blocking No. 2's man, he will make a quick break down the middle and be looking for a quick return pass. (See Diagram 48.) If it doesn't work, we just continue into our pattern of play with 2 coming off the single screen by No. 3. If the pass isn't made to 2 coming down the lane, 3 moves across behind him to become the second option. If none of the options works, we are exactly in the same position as shown in Diagram 49. In this situation, the 4 man can take a short dribble out and balance up the floor. The left side is now the strong side, the guard passes to 5 and goes to the corner to establish our BWF. (See Diagram 50.)

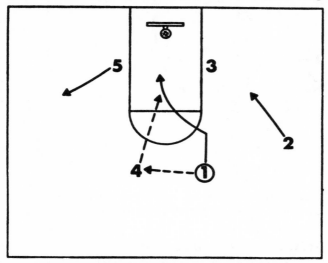

Diagram 48. Shows quick return pass to 1 from 4.

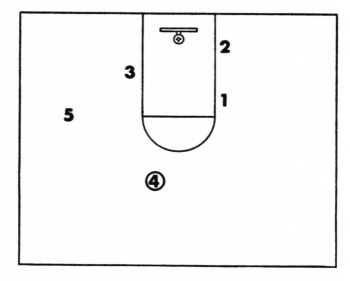

Diagram 49. Shows position of men if 4 can't feed 3 or 2.

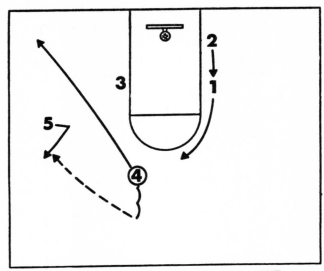

Diagram 50. Shows 4 balancing into our BWF.

REVIEW OF TEN SERIES, STRONG SIDE

Each time the No. 1 man brings the ball up the Strong Side in our Ten Series he has the three options available to him. Sometimes the defense will dictate as to what options are open to this No. 1 man. This series is just one way of getting into our Basic Working Formation but sometimes some option, as discussed, will work before our Basic Working Formation is even established. If this happens, then a shot develops very quickly and there is no need for any other passes or movement. Of the three options discussed, the pass to the No. 2 breaking out will be used far more than the other two options.

ENTER ON WEAK SIDE

If the defense is pressuring No. 1 or if for some other reason No. 1 might enter on the weak side by the 5 man breaking out and passing to him (see Diagram 51), the post just moves over and the No. 1 man goes to the corner, 2 moves in, and 4 is still our point man. Now the Left Side develops into our Basic Working Formation and our pattern of play starts from the left. The pressure of the defense on 1 usually will force 1 to go to either side. It makes no difference to us if we enter on the weak or strong side. Our pattern of play is the same from either side.

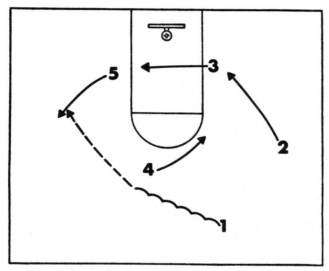

Diagram 51. Shows 1 entering on weak side.

Bring the Ball Up the Weak Side, Ten Series

Up to this time, the only thing that has been discussed is when the ball is brought up the strong side. A coach can delete the option of bringing the ball up the weak side by just moving the post over when the ball comes down the weak side. In this way, there never is the weak-side play or option.

It is much easier to move the post to get into the regular pattern and much safer than moving the ball from guard to guard. Diagram 52 indicates this move. A team can move the post over or just go into the weak-side play that will be discussed below.

When the ball is brought up the weak side of the court, the No. 1 man goes straight down the lane and blocks on the No.

2's defensive man if he attempts to come up the lane side of the center. As the No. 1 man blocks, the 2 man comes up to receive a pass from the 4 man. (See Diagram 53.) The No. 2 man should

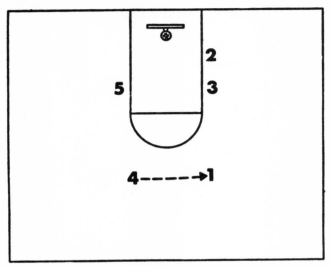

Diagram 52. Pass to be eliminated.

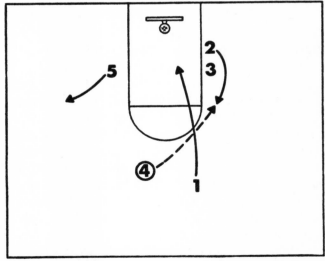

Diagram 53. Shows movement of players and ball when bringing ball up weak side.

try to run his track in close enough to pick his man on the post. If the defensive man on 2 goes to the opposite side of the center, then this is where we want the block by No. 1: We try to do three things off the maneuver: (These options are very much the same as discussed for the shot for the players in front of the double screen.)

1. Naturally, the one thing we try to do is shoot the shot in front of the post. I feel this is a real good percentage shot. If the forward does a good job of picking his man on the post, then he should be free to shoot.

2. Now, if the defensive man tries to fight through the screen on the same side as the forward, then we want the forward, if possible, to receive the pass from the 4 man and drive down the lane as in Diagram 54. We are hoping that the timing will be such that the defensive man will get himself caught on No. 3 and No. 2 will go in for a left-handed shot. The area will be cleared if 5 comes out to receive the pass from 4. Now 4 has to help clear this area by making a good fake to 5. If 5 is open, the ball can be thrown to him.

3. If the defensive man goes to the opposite side of the post as the No. 2 man, then he will get blocked by the No. 1's man, so then we try to get the shot in front of the post. Now the third thing we do at this point is have the 2 man drive back and get a short jump shot. The defensive man on 3 can, and will, shift and stop the drive to the baseline. The thing we hope to do then is get a two-on-one situation and get the ball to the No. 3 man, who gets a shot. The option we try to take in these situations is how the defensive man tries to fight the stationary screen of the No. 3 man and the moving screen by the 1 man.

One thing that should be mentioned again at this point is the movement of the No. 5 man. As we bring the ball down the weak side, we also will run our regular pattern. At about the time the 4 man is being hit by the defensive man and No. 1 is going down the free-throw lane, No. 2 is coming up the opposite side of the post, No. 5 will be coming out into position to receive a pass from No. 4. (See Diagram 54.) Now, No. 4 can move the ball to No. 5. If this is done, then 2 just comes across the lane to try to receive the pass from the opposite forward and we go into our regular pattern as discussed. Now, if the defensive man on 2 is just a little slow in fighting the screen, we get a good easy shot by the 2 man. If 5 does not receive the pass and if a shot is taken on the opposite side, we want that man to go in for the rebound.

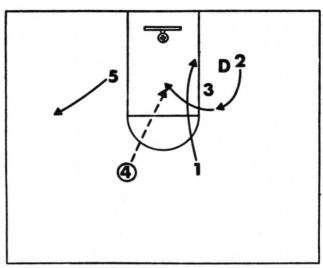

Diagram 54. Shows movement of 2 if his defensive man (D) comes up on the same side as 2.

If the ball is not moved to 2, he continues down the lane and 3 follows him across for a pass. If neither is hit by 4, we are prepared to run into our regular pattern. We should be in the position as shown in Diagram 55. As 4 takes a dribble out, 5 moves in and then out to receive the pass, 1 moves out, and 2 moves over to the weak side. Now, we are in our BWF to the left and ready to run the pattern to the left.

Now, No. 5 is the SSF and has all these options available to him:

    1.   Hit 4 in the corner.
    2.   Hit the post and split.
    3.   Move the ball to the point and become the cutter.

The quicker the team can scramble and reset into the BWF, the more effective the club will be each time it sets up for pattern.

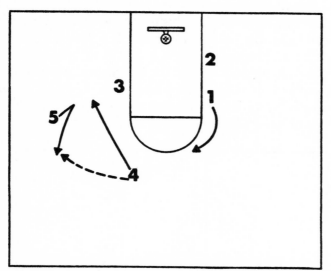

**Diagram 55. Shows position of men if 4 couldn't hit
any of his options and movement to BWF.**

TWENTY SERIES

Our entering into our Basic Working Formation is done
very quickly from our Twenty Series. We do not have all the
options and movement before entry as was discussed in the Ten
Series earlier in the chapter. The Twenty Series entry will use
both the Tandem Formations as shown in Diagrams 1 and 2. As
the No. 1 man is bringing the ball up the court, we may enter
into either the weak side or strong side of the formation. If the
No. 1 enters on the strong side, the move will be as shown in
Diagram 56.

We are now approximately in the same position as in the
Ten Series when the ball was moved to the strong side forward
and the guard went to the corner. The only difference is that
the guard and forward have exchanged positions. Now, we are
ready to run our basic pattern. All the options are available for
No. 1 that were available for No. 2:

    1.   Hit the center and split.
    2.   Hit the 4 man; now 1 becomes the cutter.
    3.   Hit the 2 man in the corner.

The big difference in the status of No. 1 (Twenty Series) and No. 2 (Ten Series) is that this man now has used his dribble once he picks up the basketball. In our Ten Series, the SSF still has his dribble. The defense now might react differently. The split to the post movement from the SSF happens much quicker in the Twenty Series than in the Ten Series. The post is usually much more open for this movement and it happens quickly so a shot can be obtained very easily.

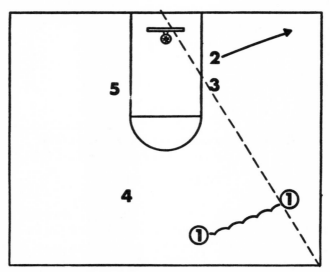

**Diagram 56. Shows No. 1 becoming SSF
and No. 2 becoming corner in BWF.**

As mentioned, the ball, when being put into play, can be entered in either the strong side or weak side. If the ball is on the weak side or if the defense forces us to the weak side when ready to put the ball into play, it is very easy to make this the strong side by just moving the post over as the weak-side forward comes out then retreats to the baseline. (See Diagram 57.) This just makes our Basic Working Formation on the left side.

If a coach desires, when entering on the weak side, he can have the No. 5 man break out, No. 1 go to the corner, and post,

No. 3, just move over. This establishes our BWF on the left side and we are in the same spots as shown in Diagram 57 but No. 1 and No. 5 have exchanged positions. One reason for this different type of entry is to get certain players in desired spots for some type of normal play or special situations.

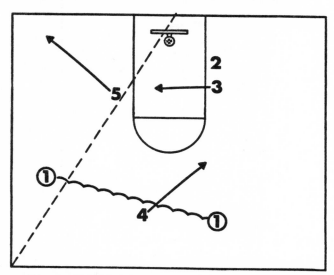

Diagram 57. Shows 20 Series entering on weak side.

THIRTY SERIES

The Thirty Series will be run from both the No. 1 and No. 2 formations. In our Ten Series of play, the No. 1 man moved the ball to the 2 man and went to the corner to establish our BWF. In our Twenty Series, the No. 1 man dribbles to the SSF position and No. 2 bounces to the corner and this establishes our BWF. Now, in the Thirty Series of play, the No. 4 man puts a moving screen for the 5 man and goes to the baseline corner on the strong side. The ball is approximately at the point and we are already in our BWF. (See Diagram 58.) Now, the 1 man has control of the play. In this series, 1 can move the ball to No. 2 breaking out or to No. 5. If the ball is moved to 5 on the weak side, we reestablish our BWF to that side—No. 1 goes to the Corner, 3 moves over, 2 becomes the Point, and No. 4 the WSF. (See Diagram 59.) If No. 1 moves the ball to No. 2, we are in our BWF immediately. For movement we want No. 1 and

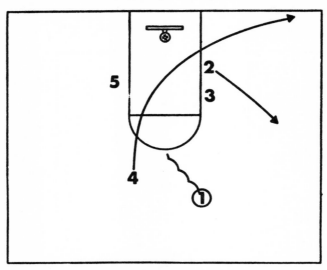

Diagram 58. Forming BWF from 30 Series.

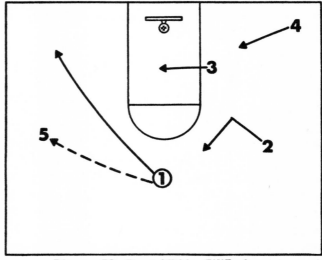

Diagram 59. Reestablishing BWF when entering weak side 30 Series.

No. 5 always interchanging on this series. The No. 2 has all options available to him as any SSF:

1. Hit the post and split.
2. Hit the corner; he may rotate or split.
3. Reverse the floor to the point.

Note: The baseline pass to the center is not good because of the movement of 4 into this area. Just as in the Twenty Series, the corner man can be hit immediately.

REVIEW OF ALL SERIES

Why the three series? Each series gives the defensive team just a bit of a different look by the placement of personnel. If one movement seems more successful than another, then the coach can instruct the team to use just that series. With the use of different series, interchanging, and rotation any player can very easily be placed at any spot on the court. It is imperative that each player learn all spots.

In any series, if the ball is entered on the weak side, the post just moves over and the Basic Working Formation is established on that side. Unless instructed, the post may set on either the right or left side and the ball usually will be entered on the strong side; but as mentioned, it makes no difference if it is entered on the weak side.

Handling Trouble Spots with the Patterned Shuffle   **3**

There are two situations that a team has to be prepared to handle if trouble occurs. These situations are:

- A. Reversing the ball from the strong side to the weak.
- B. Moving the ball to the corner, and then moving the ball back to the forward.

SITUATION (A), INTERCHANGING

As previously discussed, the strong side forward has three options after receiving the ball from the guard. One of these options is to move the ball back out to the point. (See Diagram 60.) As mentioned, we want the No. 4 man, point, to be in the center of the court when receiving the pass. If the 4 man is being pressured, then you will have trouble getting him into the correct position on the court. You then want the 4 man to block on No. 5's man and he will come out to receive the pass from No. 2. (See Diagram 61.) This puts the team in the position as shown in Diagram 62. The team is now ready to run into its pattern, but the guard works as a forward, the forward as a guard. You want each individual on your ball club to run at any position. We will make this same move many times during the course of the game even though we are not being pressured.

In this way, we are taking the defensive guards and forwards into different areas that are different to defend.

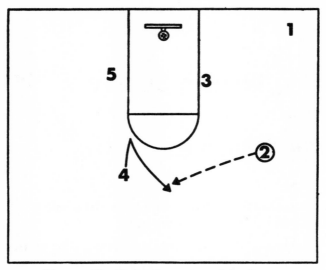

Diagram 60. Shows the option of the 2 man moving the ball to the 4 man.

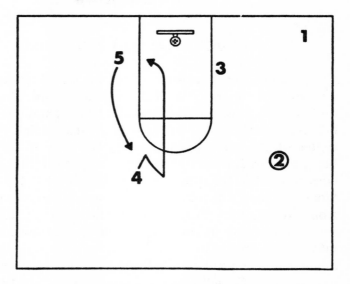

Diagram 61. Shows 4 interchanging with 5.

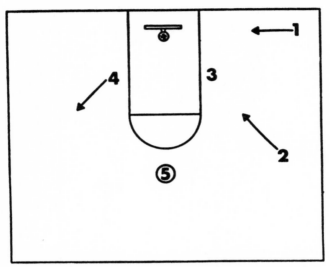

**Diagram 62. Shows position of team when 5
and 4 interchange. 5 has ball.**

We don't mind the 4 man being pressured because this then relieves one less man falling off onto the center when the 2 man is trying to hit the post. This makes it easier for us to get the ball into the post.

The V Cut

One move for the 4 man in this situation is to take his defensive man down into the lane as if to block for the No. 5 man. He then breaks out to the head of the free throw circle to receive the pass from the No. 2 man. (See Diagram 63.) The guard makes his V cut but still is being overplayed. Now, instead of just interchanging every time he continues straight out and not over. This opens the area around the key. (See Diagram 64.) Now as this happens, it alerts two people, the strong-side forward and the weak-side forward (the No. 5 man). If the strong-side forward still has not dribbled he can drive into the area for a shot or this gives us the same movement that we have discussed when driving to the top of the post in our splits.

Note the SSF can drive on the Ten and Thirty Series but that on the Twenty Series he has used up his dribble.

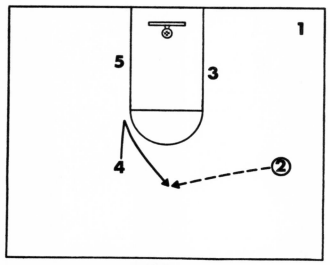

Diagram 63. Shows V cut by 4 man.

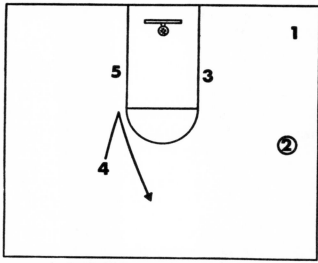

Diagram 64. Shows path for 4 man if defense is pressing the point.

The other movement or option that we like in this situation is the back door or "blind pig" which many teams have or use. This is not a called situation but a reaction situation. The WSF has the view of the entire play in front of him. If he sees the point is being pressured, this alerts him to be ready to interchange or ready to use the back door option. As mentioned, the point does his V cut but still is overplayed, so instead of going to the ball he continues straight out as shown in Diagram 64. The 5 man has to read the pressure and if he sees 4 can't receive the ball, he breaks into the opening behind the point to the ball. The point knows he can't receive the ball and he should know the 5 man is breaking up; so, as he sees the pass being made, he breaks for the basket. (See Diagram 65.) If 5 receives the ball, he now controls the game. He has the options:

1. Hit 4 breaking.
2. Hit SSF coming around.
3. Turn and shoot.
4. Drive to the outside, using post as a screen.

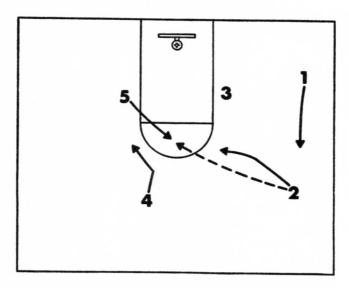

Diagram 65. Shows movement and options when 5 receives ball.

Note movement of 1 in the corner—he comes out for defensive balance. If no shots develop the team has to scramble into our BWF.

There are times when the timing will not be just right. The point may come straight out and the 5 man will break to the ball but the SSF is late reading the play. The point reads 5 but no ball has been passed. In this situation, 4 just breaks and 5 continues straight out and we interchange in this way. (See Diagram 66.) This is a good interchange movement because it makes it hard for a shift off between the 4 and 5 man.

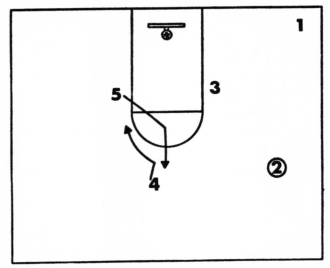

Diagram 66. Shows interchange from blind pig movement.

In teaching team defense, a coach will usually try to have the defensive man on 5 help sag on the post. This is one of the reasons for bringing out 5 fairly high when setting in the WSF position. If his defensive man is helping on the post and a team is pressuring 4, then this leaves 5 fairly open for his break. Now if a team is pressuring 5 also, then this gives us single defensive coverage on the post. If a team can handle the pressure, then this pressuring the point man is to its advantage because this opens up areas and situations that can be easy baskets or easy shots. Pressing defenses will try to keep the team from reversing the floor. This type of pressure makes it hard to run the basic offense but it does, I repeat, open up many areas at the top of the key and under the basket.

Guard Underneath

Another point to work at when interchanging the guard and forward is when teams will play zone or just switch when the interchange is being put on. The situation or play we like then is to run the guard underneath. This play has to be predetermined so everyone on the team knows it is coming. We assume at this point that the defense is pressing the point man and then switching with the interchange. We then want the 4 man to go down as if to interchange but instead get to the inside of the forward and go to the basket. The strong-side forward should move the ball to the corner and this man then hits the guard underneath. (See Diagram 67.) In this situation,

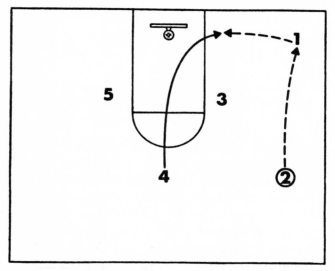

Diagram 67. Shows movement when hitting guard underneath.

we like to play the post a foot or two higher than usual. As the guard underneath is hit he looks for the shot. If this doesn't develop for some reason, he looks for the weak-side forward on the opposite side of the lane. The defensive forward gets caught with two men when the weak-side forward doesn't come out on the interchange. The strong-side forward drifts out for defensive balance. If this doesn't work, the guard just continues through to the forward's spot and we now are again in our BWF. (See Diagram 68.)

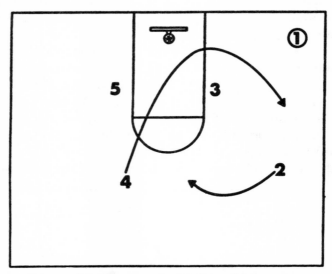

Diagram 68. Shows track of 4, if he didn't receive ball, and 2 moving out for our BWF.

I know many teams use this interchange movement so as to keep the defense moving instead of giving them a chance to sag off onto the play on the strong side. Teaching movement without the ball and teaching all the spots takes a lot of time, but interchanging is a must for these reasons: (1) It keeps the pattern moving if pressure is placed on the front line; (2) It teaches movement without the ball; and (3) In this manner, we can run any guard on to the weak side. This gives the guards the opportunity to play one-on-one on the weak side. In this manner, you can get any defensive man on the weak side and through scouting or by playing if you find a man that can beat another man one-on-one then this is a good place to work on this situation.

SITUATION (B), ROTATION

The second trouble can occur if we move the ball to the No. 1 man in the corner and then we have trouble moving the ball back to the forward. (See Diagram 69.) As mentioned in our pattern of play, we will move the ball to the corner so we can hit the post, or the guard might be free to take a shot. If

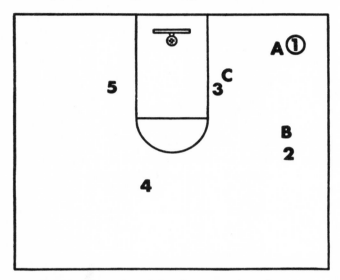

**Diagram 69. Shows defensive men a, b, and
c pressuring and 1 can't move the ball.**

neither of these options is open, the guard can then move the ball to the forward and we then can continue into the regular pattern. If we are being pressured, we just rotate the center off the post. The forward puts on a moving screen for the post, continues across the lane, and becomes the 5 man. The weak-side forward, the 5 man, rotates to the post. (See Diagram 70 for the movement.) One of the options of 1 is to hit the No. 3 man as he is breaking to the forward spot. We now are back in our BWF, Diagram 71. The center moves the ball to the 4 man, who is on the point and he then controls the pattern of play. The center is now the cutter, the 5 man is the post, etc.

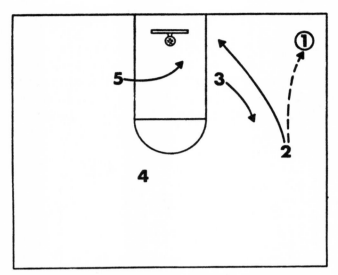

Diagram 70. Shows movement of players while
rotating with the ball in the corner.

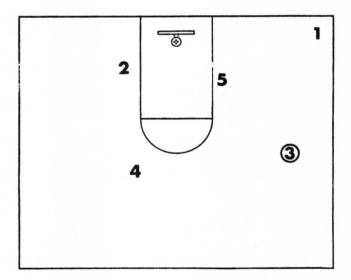

Diagram 71. Shows new position of players
in BWF after rotation is complete.

Hitting the No. 2 Man on the Rotation

I would like to state at this time that we will rotate this way occasionally, without being pressured, when we move the ball into the corner. In this way, we take the big defensive man off the post and we then also run a defensive forward who might not be as apt a defensive post man as the other post man.

One other thing that we like to do in this situation—when the ball is in the corner, have the forward get a return pass from the guard as he breaks for the basket. We have worked and passed it to this man in two ways:

1.   Hit the forward just as he breaks for the basket. There are times he makes this break right in front of the defensive man. (See Diagram 72.) It is a defensive error to allow this break but, at times when the defensive man is starting to overplay the cutter he might get free with a quick break.

2.   The other pass is for the guard to take a drive or a shot to bring his defensive man up and then pass over his

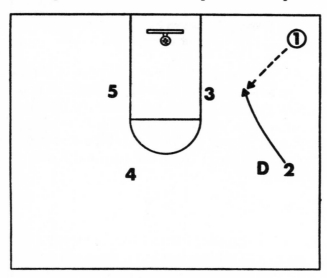

**Diagram 72. Shows one position of
hitting 2 on the rotation.**

defensive man and hit the No. 2 man later on the baseline. (See Diagram 73.) This is also a defensive error on the No. 2's man but we have found this option occasionally open. It mixes up

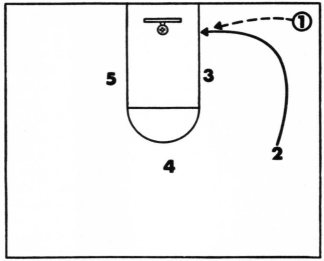

**Diagram 73. Shows 2 being hit late
with pass from the 1 man.**

very well with rotating the center off the post. A third option of the No. 1 man in the corner is hitting the No. 5 man breaking on to the post position. Now as the center receives the ball in the 2 spot, he also has the option of looking in to try to hit this man coming into the post position. This then develops into our strong-side split. The No. 1 clears the baseline, 2 goes over the top to screen, and so on.

Guard on to the Post

While on this rotation, I would like to mention one other thing that we like to do and that is run the guard into the post. We have, at times, done this when some of our guards were post men or had smaller defensive men guarding them. In either case, we like to run the guard on the post. We do this very easily by interchanging and then rotating. The No. 2 man receives the ball, moves it into the corner, rotates, looks for a return pass, as the 4 and 5 men are interchanging. (See Diagram 76.) All this movement is done very easily. We now have all four defensive men in new and different positions and are ready to run our regular pattern from BWF without much time being consumed.

A coach might want to rotate but not take the center from the post position. A team then can very easily run the outside rotation as shown in Diagram 74. If No. 2 is not hit now, No. 4 has to fill the open spot. No. 4 becomes the SSF and 5 moves up to take the point and No. 2 becomes the WSW. In this way, a team can rotate, use this movement, and still keep the post at his position.

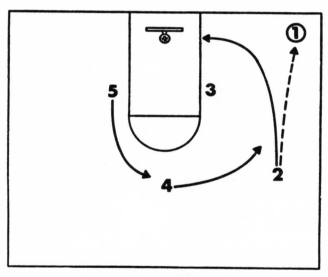

Diagram 74. Outside rotation.

Another way of filling the hole where the post leaves is to break the point into the hole. (See Diagram 75.) A reason to do this is to keep the No. 4 man, the point, moving and not standing. The SSF tries to move the ball to the point breaking out but he is pressured and the ball cannot be moved to him. A secondary pass is to move the ball to the corner, who breaks but does not receive the ball. The post breaks out and the No. 4

breaks into the post's position. The WSF, No. 5, breaks to the point and No. 2 now becomes the WSW, No. 5.

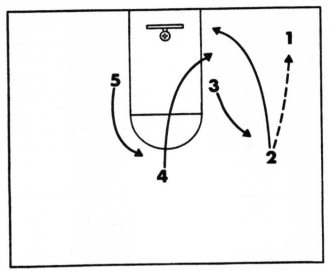

Diagram 75. Inside rotation, point filled.

The coach has to decide what rotation best fits his ball club. One of the reasons for rotation is to mismatch a smaller man on the post but this reason is not valid if the club has only one post man and he does not operate off the post. If a team has more than one post man, then this is a good way to run different men into the 3 spot.

REVIEW TROUBLE SPOTS

This past chapter has shown two trouble spots that a team will encounter in trying to move the ball. Both of these situations must be handled. A team can eliminate moving the ball to the corner, but it is a must to be able to get the ball to the point. As mentioned, if the point is pressured then this leaves a gap open around the top of the key.

Interchanging is also a must even without the pressure. In this manner, the coach can move personnel almost to any spot

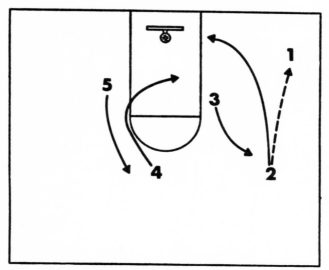

Diagram 76. Shows BWF after interchanging and rotating.

in the offense. As will be shown with the different series, rotating and interchanging each spot can be occupied with different players. It takes time to teach each spot but then it also takes time for the defense to adjust to the new defensive positions.

From a coaching standpoint, I know it takes a lot of time to teach all spots by interchanging and rotating but I also know players like both movements. They enjoy doing all this movement and playing in different spots. By doing this offensively, I believe it also teaches them how to defense different positions on the court. So when I am teaching offense, I am also teaching defense at the same time.

Using Special Plays out of the Basic Working Formation

4

At different situations, we run many plays that look much like the basic pattern. There are different ways of calling these plays out:

    A.   Call out a number when coming down the floor.
    B.   Baskets made, run a certain play.
    C.   Free throw made, run a certain play.
    D.   Out of bounds.

All special plays that we run will begin and resemble the basic pattern and start from our BWF. Any time a play doesn't work and we don't get the shot, we scramble back into our Basic Working Formation and run a basic pattern.

The one way that has been fairly successful for us in calling out a certain play is when we commit a foul. In this way, we have the whole team together. Naturally, a disadvantage is that we might not get possession of the basketball; and then again we might want to run a certain play that has been successful in that game, but a foul has to be committed before we can get organized for the play.

The way we call out the play is this: after a foul is committed our guard will call out the play to be run, while waiting for the team to get organized on the free throw lane. The football coaches give me a hard time about this because we have, at times, actually huddled before lining up on the free-throw line. This was done very easily, but the team had to hurry getting to the huddle. The man calling the play can very easily get this play from the coach by just going over to the bench.

Now as previously mentioned, we have two basic formations we can run from:

      1.   Tandem Right, No. 1 formation.
      2.   Tandem Left, No. 2 formation.

First, the guard calls the number and he then calls a letter. The first number tells us what series is to be run and the second number tells what formation is to be used. The letter gives us the play to be run. We can run plays from all three series: Ten, Twenty, and Thirty. The following examples will give some situations and plays.

    1. The guard says "11C." This means we will run from the Ten Series (first number shows this), from the 1 formation, and run the clear option. The "C" stands for the clear option that we are to run. The special plays will be shown later.

    2. The guard says "12CI." This alerts the players that we will

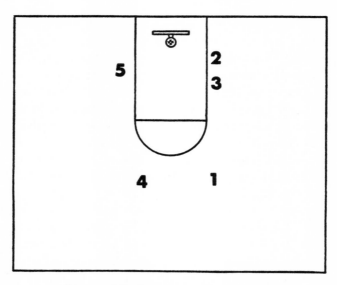

Diagram 77. Tandem right formation.

run from the Ten Series (again the first number shows this), the No. 2 tandem left formation will be used, running the clear option, and the "I" indicates that we will interchange the guard and the forward. The forward and the guard will interchange even if we are not being pressured.

3. The guard says "22C." This shows that we will run from the tandem left formation, Twenty Series, and run the clear option.

In this manner, we can run a certain play in many different ways and have different personnel running the plays. Also, this puts different personnel in different spots. We might find that one certain play works better in one game than another, so when this play is working, we want to run it many ways with different personnel in different offensive and defensive spots. Also, if we find a weak defensive man we can work on him in many situations.

STRONG SIDE CLEAR

This has been one of our most successful special plays. We can run it from any of our two basic formations and it looks and starts just like our basic pattern. I will take it from the No. 1 formation, Tandem Right Formation. (See Diagram 77.)

When we run a special play, as a general rule we do not look for any other option to run unless the defensive man makes an error or overplays us in the situation and forces us to run some other option. Usually, we revert right back to the original pattern or try to take advantage of the overplaying and freelance to get another shot.

Now, as mentioned, a free throw is being shot by the opponents, the guard has called, "11C." We definitely want the No. 1 man to bring the ball up on the strong side of the court, but if forced to we could enter on the weak side. The No. 1 man passes to the 2 man and goes to the baseline as in the regular pattern. We want the 2 man to reverse the ball right back to the 4 man. Diagram 78 shows position and movement of all men when 4 reaches and fakes the ball. The 4 man should make a good fake to the 5 man who breaks out as if to receive the pass. As the 4 man is making his fake to 5, the 3 man holds just a bit and then slides across the lane. The 2 man starts his movement of walking his man in but then comes straight across the lane. The 1 man moves along the baseline to his new position.

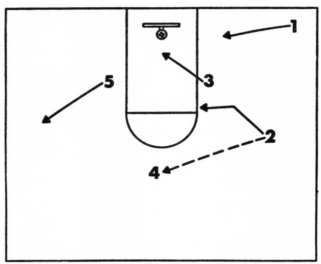

Diagram 78. Shows movement of all men on the clear.

The men should be moving into their positions or be in their positions as shown in Diagram 79 when the No. 4 man starts his drive to the right. The No. 2 man should not stop, but should provide a moving screen for No. 4 man who will attempt a pick on No. 2's man. The first option of the play is for No. 4 to drive. We hope to get a lay-up or a jump shot if his drive is stopped. The timing is usually such that the 4 man will be driving as the 2 and 3 men are moving across the lane. The second option is for the guard to stop his drive and try to hit the No. 5 man who has attempted to pick his man on the 1, 2, and 3 men. See Diagram 80 for the track of the No. 5 man. The third option is to hit the 1 man on top or near the top of the free-throw circle for the shot. The No. 1 man is the release man and he has to go to the ball. The player never knows exactly

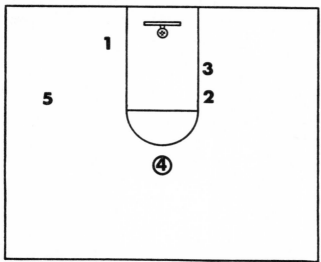

Diagram 79. Shows approximate position of men when 4 drives.

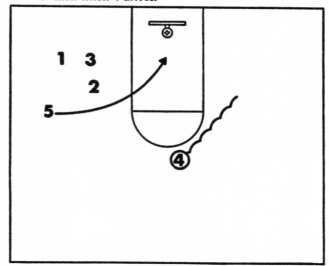

Diagram 80. Shows track of 5 man on the clear.

where No. 4 will stop the drive. See Diagram 81 for the third option.

If 1 gets the ball on the third option, and he does not get a shot we then will be in the positions as shown in Diagram 82. If none of the clear options works we have two different things we

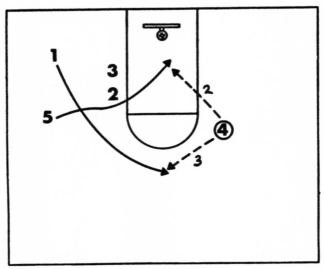

Diagram 81. Shows track of 1 and the third option of the 5 man.

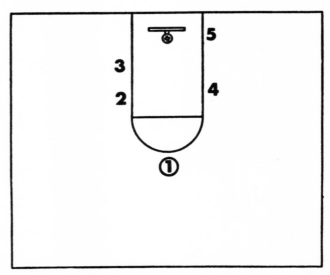

Diagram 82. Shows position of all the players if none of the three options work.

can do at this point: (A) Reset, run the clear to the other side; (B) Reset, go into pattern to the left side. A coach has to decide which of the two things he wants to run. You can't run both at the same time. In (A) the No. 1 man moves the ball to No. 2, goes to the corner, 2 passes to 4 who fakes to breaking out 5, and 4 drives to the left. Now we still have the same three options:

1. No. 4 gets a lay-up or jump shot.
2. No. 4 stops, hits 5 coming off the screens.
3. No. 4 hits 1 on top of the circle. (See Diagram 83.)

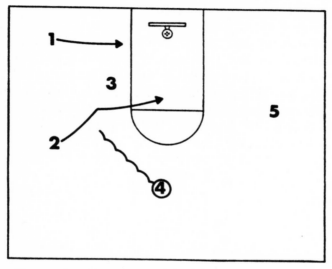

Diagram 83. Shows track of all for the clear to the left.

If a shot was not taken we are prepared then to run the clear again to the right side. There are a number of coaching points that I would like to add. The man who is running the clear must do a good job of faking to the weak-side forward when he comes out. This helps set his defensive man up for the drive. On this point, we also want to make sure that as the weak-side forward comes up he brings his defensive man out so he can be picked by our screening forward and center. We know the defensive men on 1, 2, and 3 will be shifting off on our cutter, but this then leaves someone open.

(B) If the clear option is not to be run, then we want to go into pattern. At this time, No. 2 can break out, (See Diagram 82), No. 1 goes to the corner, 3 comes to the post, and we are in our Basic Working Formation to the left side.

INTERCHANGE AND CLEAR

There are times when we feel that we know that a forward can drive his man. All we have to do then, in our calling situation, is put "I" on to the call. For example: the 5 man, the left forward, is shorter and quicker than his man. For a change, we have the guard call, "11CI." We know then that we will run the clear from the No. 1 formation, Ten Series, and the guard and forward will interchange. In this way, we have a different driver and also a different second cutter coming through for the second option. (See Diagram 84.) There are many times the defense, because of pressuring the 4 man, will force us to interchange without the call.

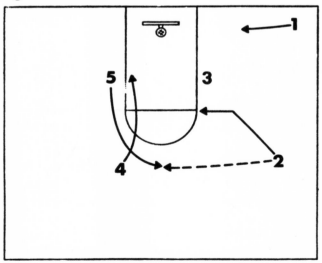

**Diagram 84. Shows position of 5 receiving ball
and preparing to run clear to the right.**

ROTATION AND CLEAR

Taking the same play but putting in a new situation, we now have the guard call, "11CR." This means we will run the clear, Ten Series, from the No. 1 formation, but first we will move the ball to the corner. We will first rotate the post and then run the clear. It works like this: the guard moves the ball to the 2 man, goes to the corner and receives a return pass from the forward; the 2 man now breaks looking for his baseline pass, center comes out to receive a pass from the guard, and the 5 man goes to the post. The positions of all men are shown in Diagram 85.

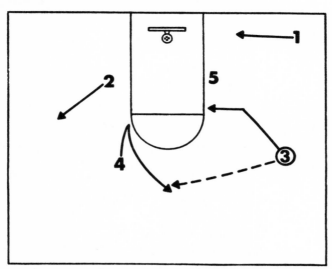

Diagram 85. Shows clear option after rotation.

OVERHEAD TO THE POST

Another situation play is the Overhead to the Post. We can run the play from either of the formations or from any of the three series. For an example, I will say that a time out has been called and we have decided to run the overhead from the Twenty Series. This play could be called "21OP." This means we use the Twenty Series, 1 formation, and the OP stands for Overhead to the Post. We are in the position shown below in Diagram 86. The No. 4 man passes to 1. The No. 1 man dribbles

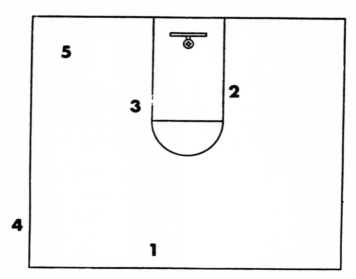

Diagram 86. 4 has ball out of bounds to start 210P.

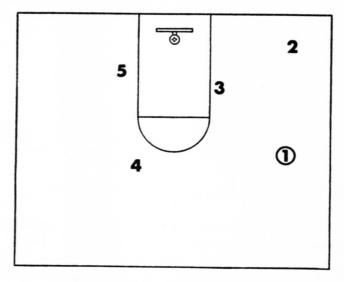

Diagram 87. Shows BWF from 20 Series.

over to become the SSF; post, No. 3, moves over with the ball. No. 2 bounces to the corner to become the corner man. (See Diagram 87.)

We are now in our Basic Working Formation to run pattern but a special play has been called. As mentioned, when a certain play has been called, we want to run that play unless the defense overplays some pass and permits us to get a shot off; but as a general rule we try to concentrate on the play as called. The No. 1 man, who really takes the place of the SSF, passes to No. 4 who, in turn, passes to the WSW, No. 5. All the basic movement is the same now as 5 receives the ball. (See Diagram 88.) The cutter hesitates in front of the post as always. In this play, he definitely takes the back track and the post rolls to the baseline and looks for a pass from No. 5. (See Diagram 89.)

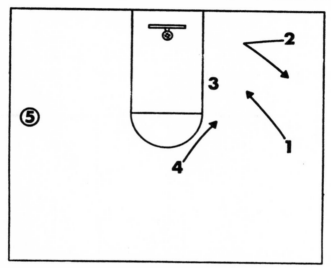

**Diagram 88. Shows basic movement
when 5 receives the ball.**

When the cutter takes the back track he tries to screen the defensive man on the post. As a general rule, the defensive man on the post will usually sag to the middle when the ball is passed to the point, the No. 4 man. (See Diagram 90.) If the timing is good, the post will roll just as the cutter clears him on the baseline side and picks on the No. 3's man. If the pass did not work, we are in the following position. (See Diagram 91.) We then scramble into our Basic Working Formation by 5

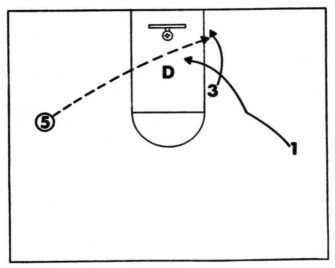

Diagram 89. Shows overhead pass to the post.

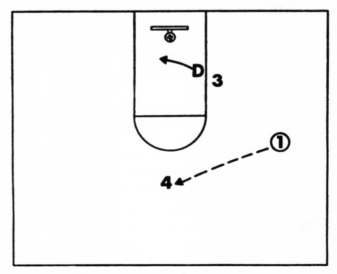

**Diagram 90. Shows movement of D-3
when ball is moved to the point.**

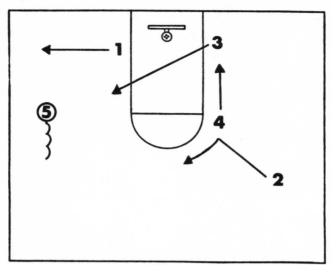

Diagram 91. Shows position if no option worked, and movement to establish BWF.

dribbling out, 1 going to the corner, post coming over, 2 to the point, and 4 dropping down to become the WSF. As always, we are ready to run into basic pattern of play from our BWF.

If the defensive team did not let us enter to the WSW and the ball had to be moved to the SSW, then the special play would be called off when passing to the SSW. If pressure is on the 4 and 5, they might interchange and the play is still run without the interchange being called. In using personnel to the best advantage, the guard may be a better passer so the team will interchange to put the best passer in this position. Also, if pressure is on, the "blind pig" may be run and this also would cancel the special situation play.

BASELINE PICK FOR THE POST

I will give the same situation that was explained for the overhead when there is a time out and the ball at half court. Now the play is called "21BP." This means we will run the Twenty Series, from the 1 formation, and the play is the

Baseline Pick for the Post. As shown in Diagram 86, 4 passes to 1, who dribbles over and we are in the same formation as in Diagram 87. Once again 1 passes to 4. Now in this situation, 4 fakes pass to 5 and then passes to No. 2 who comes out of the corner. (See Diagram 92.) Once again we try to assume that the

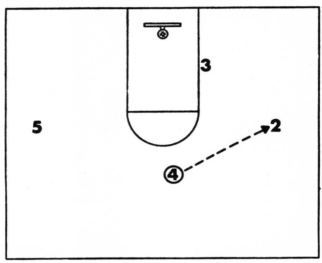

**Diagram 92. Shows approximate positions
as 4 passes to 2.**

defensive man on 3 will move as the ball is passed to 4. (See Diagram 90.) No. 1 pauses in front of No. 3 and runs the back track and tries to screen on 3's defensive man. Now No. 3 slides down right behind No. 1 and 2 passes to No. 3 with our baseline pass. (See Diagram 93.) This is the same pass we always look for when returning back to the original strong side. The only difference is that we try an extra pick by the cutter. When we know we are running this pick, we like to move the No. 3 man just a bit higher up than usual. This allows a little more room for the pass and the movement of 3. This also should bring the defensive man on the post just a bit higher. If No. 2 can't hit 3, he takes a dribble out, 5 goes to the corner, 4 to the point, and 1 becomes the WSF and we now are in our Basic Working Formation.

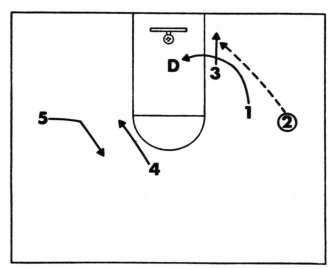

Diagram 93. Shows baseline pass to 3.

In both special plays, overhead or baseline, we can, and will, interchange without the play being called off. For example: We would like the best passer at the WSW on our overhead and also have him at the SSW on the baseline pass. If the defense doesn't allow the pass to the WSW or SSW, then we just have to reset and scramble into our Basic Working Formation.

BASELINE PICK FOR THE CORNER

This is a very quick, situation-called play that gets a shot off in front of the post. Just for convenience, let's call it "21 BC." The BC stands for Baseline Pick for the Corner.

Once again, we would be in the position as shown in Diagram 87. Now No. 1 passes to 4 and 5 comes out as to receive the pass. The corner man, No. 2, takes his man toward the basket and No. 1 now puts on a moving screen for No. 2. He, in turn, tries to receive the ball in front of the post for his shot. (See Diagram 94.) We want a moving screen by the No. 1

man. As shown, he continues to the opposite side for rebound position. Note movement of 4 and 5. Now 2 can shoot or drive back to the baseline, using 3 as a screen. If no shot develops, the team has to scramble into the Basic Working Formation. If we used the Ten Series, then the baseline pick would be for a guard.

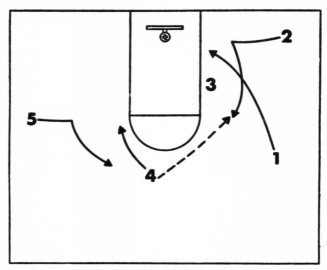

Diagram 94. Shows movement for baseline pick for corner.

REVIEW SPECIAL PLAYS

All special plays that we try to run start out to look like basic pattern from our BWF. Each play can be run from any series. Considering the series, rotation, and interchange a player can be placed in any certain spot so that the play can be set for one special player. If a situation is called, we generally try to look just for that situation but many times, due to pressure, the ball might not be moved to that spot so the situation is off. Any time we have to reset the situation, the play is called off and the basic pattern is run.

How many situation plays a team can absorb along with the basic pattern will usually depend upon the experience of the ball club. Some situation plays are better than others because of personnel. For example: The clear out is usually best for driving players while special overheads are better for taller men on the post or forward positions.

If a special play is run and no shot develops, the team has to scramble back into the basic working formation and then the basic pattern will be run.

SPECIAL CLEAR OUT FROM PATTERN

One clear-out situation has been discussed. Another clear out situation develops if the cutter is told to, or is given permission to, run our fourth track. This clear-out situation is not just a one-shot situation. It can be run any time this certain player comes to the cutter's spot. The fourth track is shown in Diagram 95. The fourth track gives a different look to our

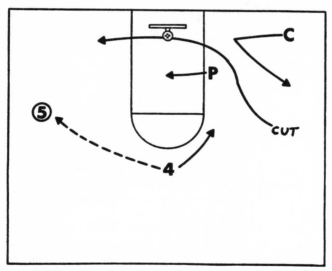

Diagram 95. Shows movement of our fourth track.

double-screen situation and as it will be shown, develops a clear-out situation.

The cutter's rule is to set opposite the post if he does not receive the ball on his shuffle cut. When the fourth track is run, the cutter continues along the baseline if he does not receive the ball. His movement is shown in Diagram 95. Now, all options are much the same for the WSW. If he hits the post, we split but the rule for a man on the baseline is to clear the baseline. The baseline drive for the WSW is eliminated. If the WSW resets, the cutter just goes to the corner, point becomes WSF, and SSW becomes the point. Now, the major change is in our double-screen option. When the SSW receives the ball and moves it to the point we now are in the position as shown in Diagram 96.

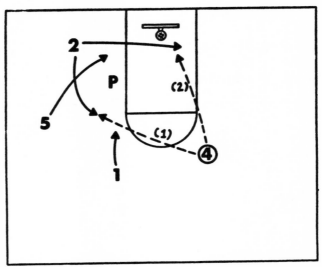

Diagram 96. Shows position and movement of all 5 men when point receives the ball.

A clear-out situation is developed for the point man and he may shoot or drive. At the same time, we are trapping and trying to box in the cutter's defensive man. The weak-side wing picks at him and the SSW goes straight down the lane to jam it up. If the clear-out man does not drive or shoot he looks for the cutter in front of the post or on the back track.

Why the different track? One of the reasons is that the cutter might be a good shooter. By the movement and blocking by the WSW and SSW, a shot can be obtained in front of the post. If the defensive man on the cutter attempts to pick his man on the post, then he runs the back-track option as shown in Diagram 96.

As mentioned, we will have just certain individuals run the fourth track. A guard may be the good shooter as well as the play maker. To develop the situation, the coach will tell the individual to run the Twenty Series when bringing the ball up the court, to be followed by running the fourth track. If nothing develops, then this man is positioned as the cutter and also is placed in the spot where he will shoot in front of the post. As explained, it is up to the coach to be able to move his players around to get the shots that are desirable for his club and players.

Setting Up a   5
Zone Offense from the
Patterned Shuffle Attack

A coach has to decide what type of shots he wants to take against any type of defense and this also prevails against zone defense. Once he decides, then he has to give his team the type of offense to make provision for getting those shots.

There are many types of zones that a team will encounter during the year. It is difficult to have a zone offense against each individual zone. Time is a big factor when coaching and teaching so it is quite difficult to do all the things that might be effective against different zones.

A zone offense should have two basic movements:

  1. Movement of the ball.
  2. Movement of the man.

The players in a zone are usually taught to defense an area in their zone. Once a man enters a zone area, the defensive man will guard him just as in any man-for-man defense. So if a man just stands in a zone area, he should be easy to defend, but a man moving in and out of an area is going to be harder to defend than one who just stays in the area. One other advantage of movement is that areas can be overloaded by movement. Different types of zones will require different overloads in different spots so if a zone offense can give this type of movement, then it should be a satisfactory offense.

We at Northern feel that we would like to try to teach basically the same offense for both man-to-man and zone defenses. As mentioned, time is quite a factor so any carry over in offenses for both types of defenses will certainly be a benefit to our teaching time.

Just as in our man-for-man offense, our zone offense has to get into our Basic Working Formation. (See Diagram 97.) The diagram shows our BWF to the right side—we also will set the same BWF on the left side.

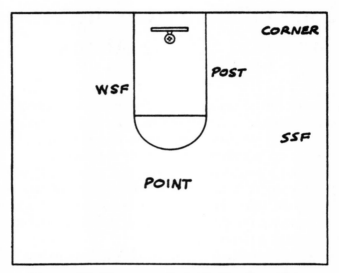

Diagram 97. Shows zone Basic Working Formation.

The following diagrams will not show any type of zones. As a coach reads through the material that follows, he can substitute the zone in which he wants the movement to fit. In this way, he can see the strong points for each movement in that zone. Each zone will react differently to the same movement. A coach will not know what this reaction will be until he plays against a particular team. He can give the basic movement that is diagrammed and then the team will have to make its own shots.

We use the same three series and both Tandem Formations to get into our Basic Working Formation:

     1.   Ten, Twenty, and Thirty Series.
     2.   Tandem Right and Tandem Left.

With the use of different series and movement, a coach can control where he wants different players, different overloads, and different screens by certain players.

A coach can give his team movement but they have to use this movement to their benefit to get the shots. Each zone will present each team with different fronts to face. The pressures the zone will force upon the offensive team will vary according to the score, type of personnel, time left in the game, and so forth. We try to get many of the same shots as in our man-for-man offense so we basically have to get into the same positions on the floor.

When the SSF has the ball in our BWF he has the same three options as in our man-for-man offensive:

1. Hit the corner, rotate.
2. Hit the post.
3. Hit the point.

Hit the Corner

If the ball is moved to the corner, he has the options to shoot or move the ball to the post. Now the post can shoot or move the ball out to WSF, point, or back to the corner for a shot. Here again the zone determines what openings will develop.

Hit the Post

The post is still the center of our offense against all zones. It is harder to get the ball inside but this option prevails when the No. 2 man has the ball. If the post is hit by the SSF he may shoot or move the ball out to any of the perimeter men, WSF, point, or corner.

Hit the Point

As in our man-for-man offense, we want the point to receive the ball in the middle of the court. If he is pressured on this pass, he must come straight out to receive the ball. Once he receives the ball, we like the point man to try to penetrate inside the zone. (See Diagram 98.) How far he can dribble into

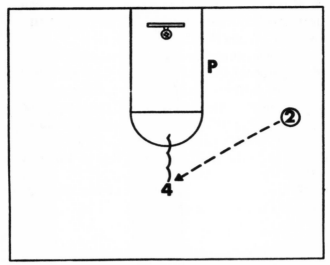

**Diagram 98. Shows point man trying
to penetrate into zone.**

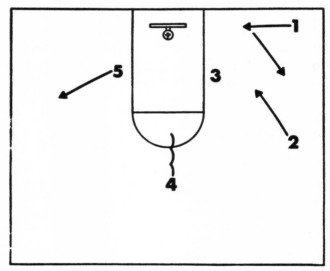

Diagram 99. Shows movement when point receives ball.

the zone will depend upon the type of zone. Against a one man
front zone, he will be challenged quickly but against a two man

front that challenge shouldn't be as quick. This dribble will draw the defensive wing men in and then the pass to the wings won't have to be as wide as if these two defensive men had not been drawn in. The point man has the options of shooting, hitting the post, or hitting either wing. The players have to see what options are open to him on just the dribble and then take advantage of these options. When the point receives the ball, we still have the same basic movement of the cutter and both wings. (See Diagram 99.)

WEAK SIDE WING'S OPTIONS

As mentioned, the point can move the ball to either wing. Our options of the WSW are much the same as in our man-for-man offense:

1.   Hit the cutter.
2.   Hit the post.
3.   Shoot or drive.
4.   Double screen.
5.   Reset.

Where each option is open will vary according to the type of zone. Our cutter has a bit more movement in the zone than in man-for-man, but basically, the same type of rule as resetting opposite the post still prevails if nothing develops. Before setting opposite the post, the cutter will sometimes go along the baseline on the side of the WSW and the post comes across as the second option. This track is like our fourth track discussed in our chapter on special plays. We now have an overload on the side of the ball with the WSW in charge of the play. Note in Diagram 100 that the point and the SSW moved the same as in our man-for-man movement.

How the zone will react to the overload can't be determined. The ball may be moved to the cutter who can shoot or hit the post. The WSW might shoot. As the point goes away from the ball, he sees that the cutter goes along the baseline for the overload as shown in Diagram 100. The point man should then continue down the lane into rebound position as shown in Diagram 101. Now he is in good rebound position if

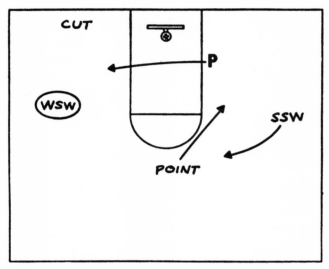

**Diagram 100. Shows cutter on baseline and
also shows movement of point and SSW.**

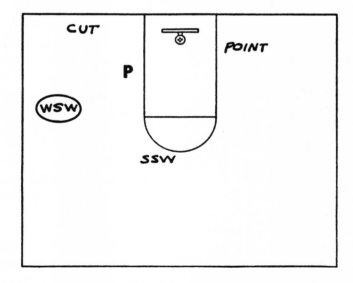

Diagram 101. Shows lower position of point.

cutter or WSW shoots. He is also in position to receive an overhead pass from the WSW and if the post is hit, then he is a

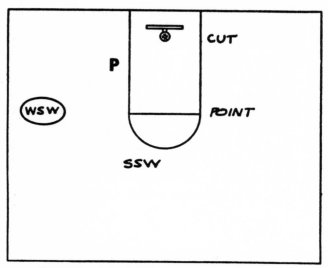

Diagram 102. Shows position of all 5 men
when cutter resets opposite post.

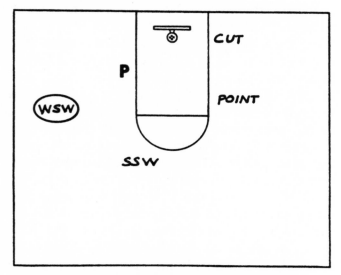

Diagram 103. Position of personnel
when cutter takes baseline track.

good release option for the post. If no options develop from this movement, then the cutter comes back along the baseline to reset opposite the post. The point moves up to his normal positions about free-throw-line high. (See Diagram 102.) Now WSW can still go into the double screen situation or reset option. Both of these options will be discussed later. Sometimes, the cutter will take the baseline track and the post will come across by himself. We then are immediately in the following position as shown in Diagram 103. The options are the overhead, the shot by the WSW, or the pass to the post. Once again, the player has to find the opening. If the cutter does not come, then this leaves the baseline open for a quick drive. Once again the reaction of the zone to the movement cannot be determined. Note the good position of two rebounders if WSW shoots.

DOUBLE SCREEN

After the point moves the ball to the WSW, he goes away from the ball as has been shown in the preceding diagrams. When the point goes away, he blocks on some man. Again, this will vary as to whom because of different defenses. The SSW comes hard to the ball just as in our man-for-man offense. If the block is successful by the point, then the SSW gets a lot of shots in front of the screen. Note good rebounding positions of the cutter, post, and WSW going in for his new movement. (See Diagram 104.) Once again, this movement will vary according to the zone defense. The above double-screen option developed very quickly for the WSW. He hit the SSW immediately as the point blocked and the SSW came into position. The double-screen situation and the movement that will be shown below still can be used in the delay option of the WSW. This delay option double screen could come from the movement shown in Diagram 102 and 103. In this delay movement, the WSW looked for other options. Nothing developed from the overload by the cutter on the baseline so now he still can go into the double-screen situation. Sometimes, we will get into the double-screen movement quickly and other times it will be delayed.

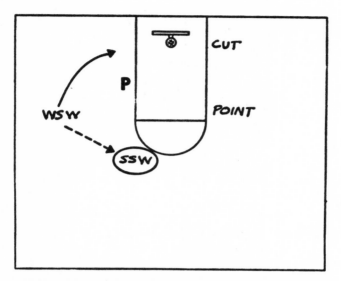

Diagram 104. Note rebounding strength if shot is by SSW.

    If no shot is taken by the SSW, he then moves the ball to the point. Here, again, many shots will develop. If the zone has a one-man front, we now have a two-on-one situation established. At this time, the point controls the options. He may shoot, hit the post, move ball back to SSW, or hit WSW behind the post. Note the good rebound position if point shoots. If nothing develops, we now want the cutter to break for the ball. (See Diagram 105.) The lower the cutter can receive the ball, the better but once again the defense will dictate this pass. The cutter now has the options of shooting, hitting the WSW coming across low on the baseline, hitting the post coming across high, or hitting the SSW with an overhead pass. Note the movement of the SSW down the lane the same time as the WSW moved over. (See Diagram 106.) *Repeat:* The player has to find the openings and these will vary as to the type of zone played and movement of defensive men in it.

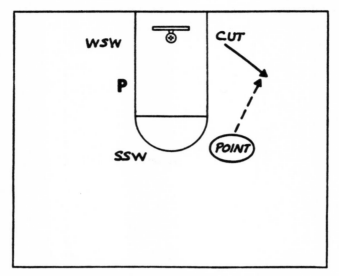

**Diagram 105. Shows position when
                cutter breaks for the ball.**

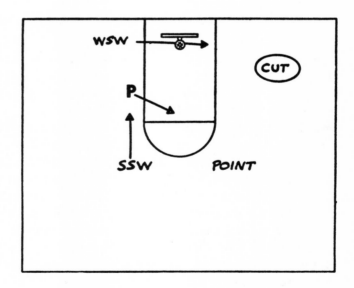

**Diagram 106. Approximate movement
                when cutter receives ball.**

PLACEMENT OF PERSONNEL

At this time, I would like to talk about placement of personnel in the zone. The cutter and the post could be the best two rebounders. If the cutter is a better rebounder than a shooter, then we want him to take the baseline track and let the post come across the lane toward the WSW. If a shot develops, then the cutter is in good rebounding position. If no shot develops, we still come into the double-screen situation in which the SSW or the point can shoot. The cutter is still in good rebounding position. If nothing develops we are in position as shown in Diagram 107.

Now a change in movement can be made if a coach wants to keep the cutter in position as shown in Diagram 107. As mentioned, nothing developed for the point. Now, instead of having the cutter break out, the WSW breaks across, the cutter picks on the baseline defensive man. (See Diagram 108.) What develops depends upon the zone and its movement. The WSW

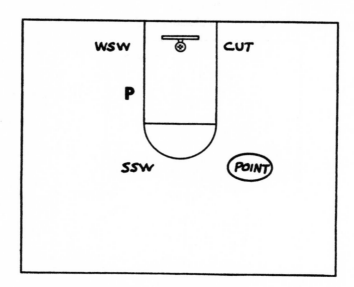

Diagram 107. Shows position of all 5 men on
double screen when point has the ball.

now has the options of shooting, hitting the cutter inside, post coming across high, or hitting the overhead to the SSW. (See Diagram 109.) The post would not come across until the WSW

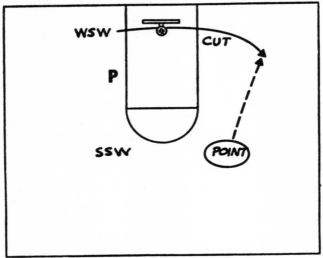

Diagram 108.   Shows WSW breaking across low and cutter in blocking position.

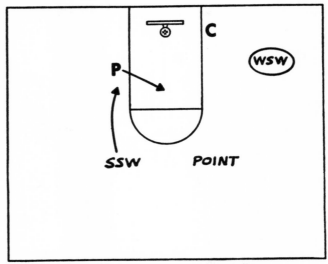

Diagram 109.   Shows approximate movement of all men when WSW receives ball.

has the ball and the SSW would go down the lane about the same time the post starts across the lane. If nothing develops at this time, the WSW dribbles out and the team has to scramble back into its BWF just as it does in the man-for-man offense. I have found that once nothing develops a team has to get reset and start its movement and get its rhythm back into its movement.

BACK TO THE ORIGINAL STRONG SIDE

The point, when receiving the ball from the SSF, has the options of moving the ball to the WSW or SSW. The options and movements of the WSW have been discussed. If the point moves the ball to the SSW, we are approximately in the positions as shown in Diagram 110. Note movement of point and WSW. In Diagram 110, the cutter is in position if he took the baseline track. If he took this track and stayed, the cutter may break down the baseline and we now have an overload on the right side of the court. The SSW can hit the post, shoot, or move the ball to the cutter on the baseline. What shots develop now on

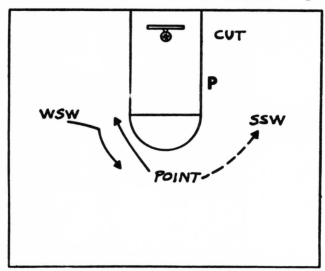

**Diagram 110. Shows approximate position
if SSW receives the ball.**

this overload depends upon how each defense reacts to the movement. If no shots develop, I want a reset to our BWF and another start with our basic movement.

CUTTER SETS OPPOSITE THE POST

Once again, if the cutter is a good rebounder, we want him to set opposite the post when the ball comes back to the original strong side. (See Diagram 111.) The SSW still has his options to drive, shoot, or hit the post. If nothing develops, the double-screen situation is now our next try for a shot. (See Diagram 112.) The first option for the WSW is to shoot. Note cutter, post, and SSW in good rebounding position. If no shot develops for the WSW, he then can hit the point. Once again, we should remember that the point blocked someone when going away from the ball—who is blocked depends upon the type of defense. The point has the options of shooting, hitting the post, hitting the SSW, or moving the ball back to the WSW. Some defenses have only one man guarding the point and WSW and with the movement of these two men into the double-screen

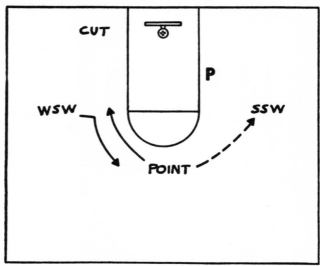

**Diagram 111. Cutter, good rebounder,
sets opposite the post.**

situation many shots can develop by just these two men. If no shots are taken, then the cutter breaks out and he now controls the play. (See Diagram 113.) If the cutter shoots, note good

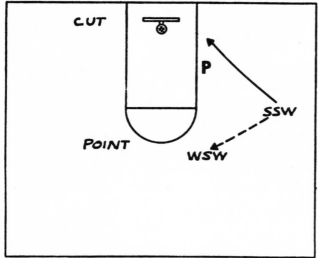

Diagram 112. Shows positions when
double screen is developing.

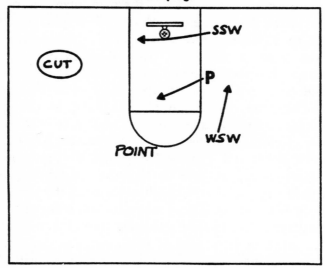

Diagram 113. Shows movement as
cutter receives the ball.

rebounding position of SSW, post, and WSW. If nothing develops, the team should scramble back into its BWF and start its movement once again.

CUTTER REBOUNDER

If, in Diagram 113, the Cutter is a good rebounder and the SSW is a better shooter, then the SSW goes along the baseline to receive the ball and the cutter tries to pick the defensive baseline man. (See Diagram 114 for movement.) Now the SSW can shoot. Note rebounding strength of cutter, post, and WSW. The SSW can look in on the cutter, hit the post coming across, or hit WSW with an overhead pass. If nothing develops, the SSW has to dribble so that the team can scramble back into its BWF and start over again.

REVIEW ZONE OFFENSE

By moving the ball and the men, many overloads develop against the zones. These overloads will develop in different areas due to different types of zones. The double-screen movement gives some of the same basic shots as in the man-for-man offense. Both wings should receive the ball in approximately the same spot on the court, free-throw-circle high. A team has basically the same type of movement as our man-for-man offense so the learning situation is not as time consuming as if a new offense had to be completely installed. The terminology of series, BWF, and Tandem formations are the same so this also helps in conserving time to teach the options that are developed with the movement. A coach cannot tell the players where the shots will develop. The movements will make the openings and the players have to see these openings and then react.

Another advantage of the same basic movement for both zone and man-for-man is that some teams will change their defenses during a game. There are teams that will vary their defenses down the court each time. This makes a confusing situation for the offensive team as to what defense the team is in but if their basic movement is the same for each defense then a team doesn't have to decide what offense to run.

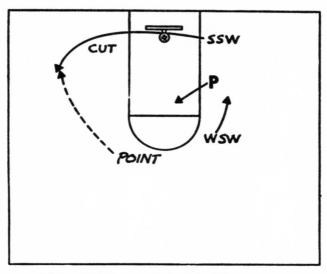

Diagram 114. Movement when SSW goes along baseline and cutter holds.

Coaching a Delay Offense from the Basic Working Formation

6

There are times during games when a coach wants to hold onto the ball and slow up the game. When a coach does this, a team doesn't want to quit shooting but wants to take just the real percentage shot. In our slow-up game, we try to use the same basic movement but eliminate some of the shots that we normally would take. Some of the basic shots eliminated are shots from the wings and shots from the double-screen situations. All a coach has to say is that we are in our delayed offense and then those shots will not be taken.

WSW OPTIONS

In our delayed offense, the movement is basically the same until a certain point is reached. We get into our BWF the same way, the movement of the ball to the point is the same, and the movement after the ball is moved to the wings is the same. If the point moves the ball to the WSW, then his option of shooting is removed. We always are looking for the cutter or the post. If the post is hit, we split but no shots are taken by other than the post—in other words, no out shots. The reset is still there and the drive is satisfactory but still, only shots that are on the board are acceptable. I feel a team shouldn't quit taking the ball to the board. The one situation that is really changed for the WSW is our double-screen situation. If he doesn't hit the cutter or the post, doesn't drive or reset, we then are in the following positions as shown in Diagram 115. Now, the SSW comes to the double-screen situation as in regular pattern but his track might be a bit flatter than his regular track. (See Diagram 116.) As the SSW goes in front of the defensive man on the point, the point man breaks to the top of the key to receive a pass from the WSW. The SSW continues straight across the lane and sets next to the post. (See Diagram 117.) The point

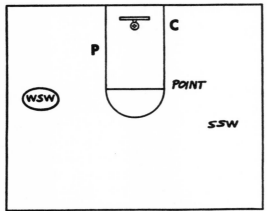

**Diagram 115. Position of players
if WSW didn't hit any options.**

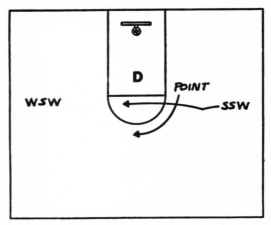

Diagram 116. Shows flatter track of SSW.

now moves the ball to the cutter breaking out. The cutter now is concentrating on two basic options:

1. Hit the WSW.
2. Hit overhead pass to SSW.

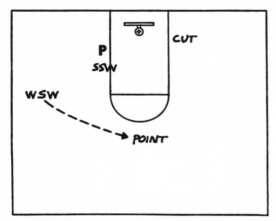

**Diagram 117. Shows position of players
when the point receives the ball.**

Hit WSW

The WSW in this situation will always take the back track. The cutter's main option is to hit this man so he can get the lay-up shot. (See Diagram 118 for this back track.)

Hit the SSW

The other option of the cutter is to hit the overhead pass to the SSW. The defensive man who will stop this double-screen option of the WSW is the defensive man on the post. He should be able to see this option materialize. The offensive post's duty in this delay offense is to screen on the SSW's man. Now he does not know where this defensive man will be so his moves will be dictated by the position of the defensive man. He can be basically in two positions in the lane in relation to the post, higher or lower. (See Diagram 119.) If the man is about in Position (1), fairly high, then the post man will use his right foot as his pivot foot and drop his left foot into the lane. This then puts his back to the basket and he faces (1) for his block. The SSW then rolls to the basket looking for the pass from the cutter.

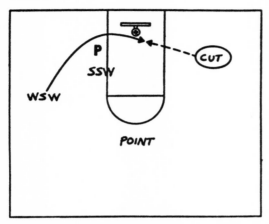

Diagram 118. Shows back track for WSW.

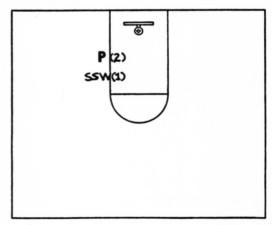

Diagram 119. Shows two possible positions of defensive man on SSW.

The defense man at times will drop into a fairly low Position(2). If the defensive man is in this position, then the post man will again use the right foot as the pivot foot but will face the basket and try to screen (2) by getting him on his back. Once again, the SSW rolls to the basket and the ball. The timing should be fairly quick. As soon as the WSW clears the post to the inside, the offensive post should be pivoting to block on the SSW's man and the SSW rolls to the basket. In our controlled offense, the post comes across as an option, but he is not the main option. If no option is hit, we are in position as shown in Diagram 120. *Note:* In the delay game, the point does not go

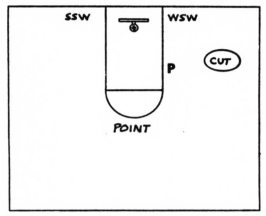

**Diagram 120. Position of players
if no option is hit.**

away from the ball when he hits the cutter, who was a wing. If nothing developed, the cutter takes a dribble out, WSW goes to the corner, and the post, point, and SSW are all in our BWF. From this position, we are ready to try again.

Hit the SSW

The point can always move the ball to either wing in our delay offense. If the SSW is hit by the point, then he controls our play. First, the SSW looks for the baseline pass to the post or he may drive but only board shots are being looked for in this option. If the post is hit, he can shoot (but no shots from the split movement and no shots by the SSW). Just like the WSW delay play, we now have the SSW play from the double-screen movement. When the point's defensive man is screened by the WSW coming into the double-screen position, we want the point to move to the top of the lane to receive the pass from the SSW. (See Diagram 121.) As soon as the ball is moved to the point, the SSW should try to walk his man into the double screen set by the WSW and post. The SSW takes the back track and looks for the pass from the cutter who has received the ball from the point. (See Diagram 122.)

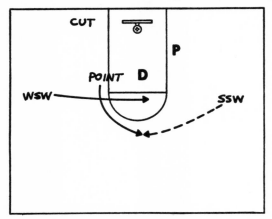

Diagram 121. Shows track for WSW and point.

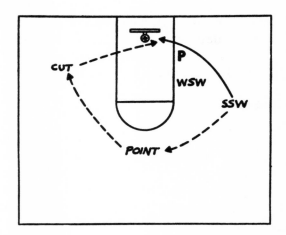

Diagram 122. Shows track for the SSW.

This track is a much sharper and quicker track than when running just as a basic cutter. The post looks for the defensive man on the WSW. He will usually be in one of the two spots shown in Diagram 123. If the defensive man is high, as in (1)

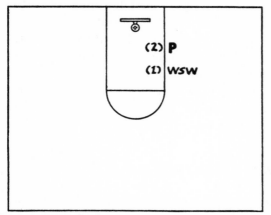

Diagram 123. Shows two positions of defensive man on WSW.

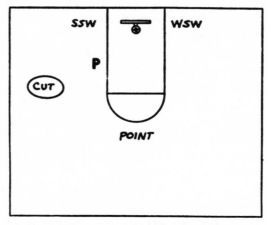

Diagram 124. Shows position of players if no shots developed from two options of cutter.

position, the post will pivot on his left foot in the lane and have his back to the basket. There is a slight pause on the screen as the WSW rolls to the basket. After the pause, the post continues across the lane. If the defensive man (2) slides low into the lane, the post man again pivots on his left foot but pivots so he faces the basket and tries to get (2) on his back. He pauses on the screen, SSW rolls to the basket, and the post continues to go to the ball. If no shots develop, we are in the position shown in Diagram 124. Now the cutter takes a dribble out, SSW to the corner, and the post, point, and WSW fall into position in our BWF. What options the cutter, who is the 2 man in our BWF, wants to initiate is up to him. He may move the ball to the corner, rotate, or move the ball to the point and become the cutter.

REVIEW THE CONTROL GAME

In a control game, a team should be trying to score and not just hold onto the ball. The movements described above can be run twice through in about 30 seconds of play. A lot of passes are made but they are short and crisp, and if the timing is good, the point man can get the ball in very good position if he times his break just as one of the wings clears his defensive man. Now the point concentrates on just getting the ball to one of the wings. If this pass can't be made, the point has to take a dribble and the team has to scramble into our BWF.

In the delayed game, if the defense is pressuring, it opens up the options of the cutter and also the option of the baseline pass from the SSW. These options are always looked for when running pattern. The biggest change from basic pattern is the double-screen situation.

It is up to the coach to give his team the type of movement he wants to try to control the game and it is up to the players to execute the proper passes. Naturally, teaching shot discipline is a must in the delay game. It is hard for a player to pass up shots that were considered good shots in the earlier part of the game.

Movement and
Player Placement for
the Patterned Shuffle

7

A coach should know the strength and weaknesses of his players. He should also know where he would like to place his personnel in his offense. The defense, however, by pressuring, will dictate to him the limitations of the placement of this personnel. A point I would like to mention at this time is the position of the post. In our tandem formations, right or left, we will vary as to how high the post or No. 3 man will set. If we are not being pressured, we like to set a very low post.

This low post position takes away the areas for a cutter but then it opens up the areas for our double-screen shots. These shots will develop much closer to the basket. Another shot that develops quickly is the shot when bringing the ball down the weak side; in the Ten Series, this is the shot for the SSF in front of the post. The No. 1 goes inside the post, blocks for No. 2 who gets the shot in front of the post. (See Diagram 125.) This is very simple and easy to execute if little pressure is put on the 4 man and the post is set low. One pass and the shot is taken.

If we are being pressured, we like to bring the three front men out a bit higher and run our offense higher on the court. (See Diagram 126.) For the higher post position, the one thing the defense takes away from the club is the percentage shot over the post when bringing the ball down the weak side, but then it opens things up under the basket for a drive across the middle or the drive back to the baseline. The one thing this really opens up is the area under the basket for the shuffle cutters. It also opens up the baseline pass to the post. The more

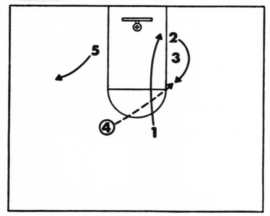

Diagram 125. Low post.

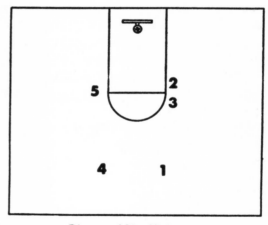

Diagram 126. High post.

the defense pressures each spot, the better because this gives the players more opportunities to get the ball into the post. It is impossible to pressure and also sag. If the ball club can handle the pressure, then this pressure works for the club because it creates openings that a sagging defense won't create.

If a team is pressuring No. 2, then there are a few maneuvers that can be used to try to free him. One is to take his man right up to the 3 man so that they are tight against each other. (See Diagram 127.) Now the defensive man has to be to the inside of No. 2 or behind him and 2 should be able to get in good position for the pass without an interception. From this same maneuver, we can break out the No. 3 man for the pass and then 2 just stays on the post. (See Diagram 128.) It is a

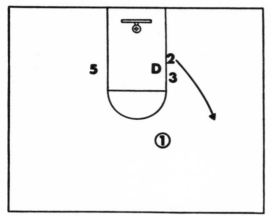

Diagram 127. Shows tight position of No. 2.

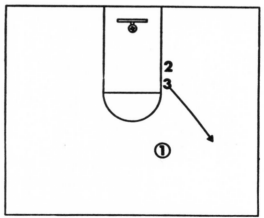

Diagram 128. Shows 3 breaking out into the 2 spot.

talking situation between the two men who will come out to receive the ball from the No. 1 man. This is an easy way to take the big defensive man away from the post position. This same move can be made from just the normal positions of the 2 and 3 men but it is harder to coordinate the moves of 2 and 3; but in this way, the big defensive man just can't slide off into the other man. Also, in this position, the big man doesn't pressure the pass into the strong-side forward as well as a smaller man.

One other maneuver that can be used at times is for the 2 man to screen for the 5 man. In this way, they just interchange positions. (See Diagram 129 for this movement.) Although this is not a tough maneuver, it does take good timing so that the 5 man comes into position when the 1 man is ready to move the ball in to the forward. Right along with this maneuver, the 2 man can just fake his move as if to block and then come out to receive the pass. I would like to emphasize again that we do not want the No. 2 man too high up on the court or too wide. The closer he can be in towards the center, the better for feeding and the better position he will be in to shoot if the defensive man sags off on the center.

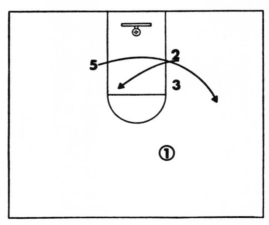

Diagram 129. Shows 2 blocking for the 5 man.

The same maneuver mentioned in Diagram 129 can also be used when bringing the ball up the weak side of the court by the No. 4 man. The timing in this situation is hard to work on but it does free the No. 5 man for the shot. Once again, I repeat that all of these movements cannot be learned at the same time. Each one can be added as the need arises or as the team progresses.

TANDEM LEFT

In the previous pages, the pattern was discussed only from the Tandem Right Formation. As stated before, no one knows what formation will be used each time the team comes down the court unless a specific situation has been called to use a certain formation.

Now in setting up in the Tandem Left, as shown in Diagram 130, we use the same movement entirely. If the ball comes down the strong side of the court, Ten Series, the guard has the same three options.

1. Hit the strong-side forward.
2. Hit the center.
3. Hit the weak-side guard.

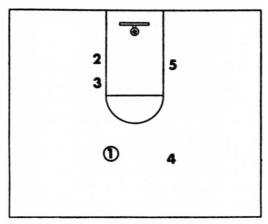

Diagram 130. Tandem Left Formation.

As previously mentioned, there is no sequence as to the order to the above options that can be hit. Repeat—the defense does dictate as to what pass is open.

If the strong side forward, No. 2 man, is hit, then he also has the same movement and options as the strong side forward in the Tandem Right Formation:

1.   Look at the post.
2.   Hit the No. 1 man in the corner and rotate.
3.   Reverse the floor to the No. 4 man.

Once again, there is no sequence as to options two or three.

If the ball is brought down the right side, which is the weak side, then we go right into the weak-side play.

As a general rule, the players do not know which side will be the strong or weak side. This, then, makes it imperative that recognition as to these be automatic. Getting to the proper spots on the floor, and then reacting with the proper movements, takes a great deal of practice.

If the team and players come down the floor slowly, it is easy to set up and make the proper movements. But when things get disorganized and a team comes down more quickly, as in the break, then recognition makes it a tougher job to get set up in the formations to start into the pattern of play.

REVIEW

The above shows the two basic formations that we use in getting into our regular pattern of play. The numbers that are used in the diagrams are used only to help follow the sequence of the pattern. For example: When 4 interchanges with 5, then in theory 5 becomes the weak-side guard and 4 the weak-side forward. If 3 comes off the post instead of 2, then these two men in theory have exchanged numbers. In other words, a player assumes the duty and movement of the position he is in or comes to from another position. As it has been shown, a player can be a guard, forward, and a center all in just a few movements. It is imperative that, in this type of shuffle offense, each player be capable of running each spot or position on the court.

The success of any basketball team depends on its fundamental abilities on defense, offense, and the all-important thing, desire to play. Along with the above-mentioned, the success of the pattern depends upon how all of the players are able to run each numbered position. In this way, we can run the same pattern with different defensive men defending different positions. Also in this manner, we can take a defensive man into any position that we want him. The success of the play then depends on the players being able to take the advantage, once a defensive man is in a different position.

The success of any pattern or play also depends on the ability of each player to free-lance or take an advantage of any defensive error that an opponent commits. A player must control the pattern and not the pattern control the player.

The Shuffle Offense can be used in its entirety if, and only if, each player learns all positions. If a team has one good post man and does not want to take this man off the post, then rotation is just eliminated from the offense but it is a must that the other players learn the other four spots.

Each team a coach has will have different types of players. Some will be shooters and not drivers. Others are drivers, not shooters. A club may have one person who is outstanding, so then he has to position this one player to give him many opportunities to score.

Example: A guard is the one man to bring the ball up the court and also a good driver and play maker of the team. What

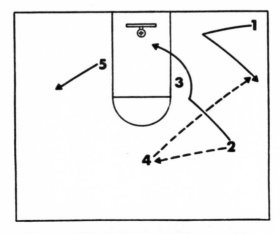

Diagram 131. Back to original strong side.

is one of the best ways I can try to use this player? I can have him bring the ball up the court, Ten Series, pass to the SSF, go to the corner; the SSF moves ball to the point, cutter goes through and the point moves the ball back to the SSW. Now, this good guard has half the court and the post to work with to try to score. (See Diagram 131.)

Example 2: The guard, ball handler and shooter, brings down the basketball, Thirty Series, moves ball to No. 2 man—interchange with the 5 man. The ball is moved to 5 and over to the guard at the WSW position. This man now can use his talents—pass to cutter or post, drive or shoot. (See Diagram 132.)

Example 3: A forward is a good driver. Situation: Use Twenty Series, interchange, and with one pass to the forward, using the clear play; the forward now has the opportunity to play one-on-one at the top of the key. (See Diagram 133.)

Example 4: A forward is a good shooter. Situation play—Twenty Series. The ball is moved to the point who now goes down and blocks for the forward who was the corner man. This is called the baseline pick for the forward. (See Diagram 134.)

Example 5: A forward and center are about the same size and both handle themselves at the post position. Place them both together at the 2 and 3 spots in Tandem formation. Now,

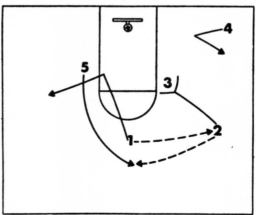

Diagram 132. 30 Series and to weak side.

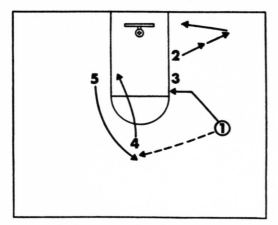

Diagram 133. Interchange, 20 Series Clear.

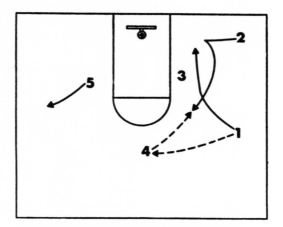

Diagram 134. Baseline pick 20 series.

the man with the smaller defensive man stays in the post, creating a mismatch on the post. This same mismatch can be created by rotation. (See Diagram 135.)

Example 6: The guard is the good passer. Delayed Offense—Twenty Series, with good guard as cutter. The ball is moved to either wing; nothing develops for the wing the ball was passed to. Now, the opposite wing comes into double-screen situation as explained. The point breaks out, receives ball, passes to good guard who is now on the weak side. The good passer now can feed cutter or overhead. (See Diagram 136.)

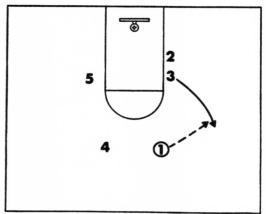

Diagram 135. Shows breaking big man to spot.

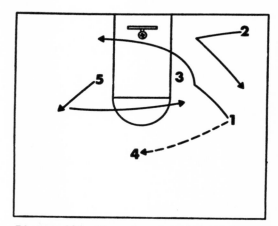

Diagram 136. Shows how to get good passer in position on delayed offense.

The above examples are just a few situations of placing players to utilize their abilities. The coach can manipulate and move his personnel about to the best advantage only if he understands the offense, and then he also must know the limitations of his players.

Drills for Teaching the Patterned Shuffle Attack

8

The question that comes into a coach's mind when teaching an offense such as the shuffle is how much time will be involved in learning the offense. I know from experience that each boy and each club will learn at a different rate. I know the offense can be taught on the high school level as well as on the college level. I feel that each player should try to learn all spots early and then try to specialize in positions. The drills given below are designed to teach each spot.

When teaching basic pattern, the movement has to be drilled many, many times before it is completely controlled and learned by the players. The basic steps in teaching any offense are:

1. Drill movement and options without a defense.
2. Drill movement and options with a skeleton defense.
3. Half-court work with passive defense.
4. Half-court work with tough defense.
5. Full-court scrimmage.

Our basic drill for teaching our movement and technique is our Scramble Drill shown in Diagram 137. The formation starts out as our Basic Working Formation. I want the 3 man to have the ball. Now 3 moves the ball to 2 and we are ready to teach any phase of our offense.

Note: Emphasize 2's straight line position; post end basket.

Example: We are just teaching the Baseline Track for the Cutter, no. 2. Now 2 passes to 1, who passes to 5 who in turn hits the overhead to the cutter. I want 1 and 4 also running their track at the same time.

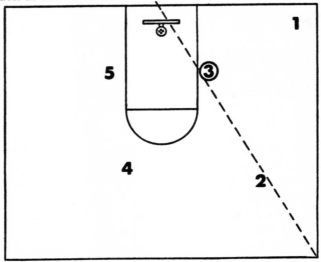

Diagram 137. Shows position of players for Scramble Drill.

In working the drill above, I like to have another part of the squad under another basket. The first unit works on the option being taught, completes it, and then the second unit completes the option. Now while the second unit is working, then the first unit scrambles into new positions. As soon as the second unit is finished, then the next unit executes the option but everyone is in a different spot on the court. Naturally, the second unit is scrambling to new spots while the first unit is executing. Each time a coach wants to teach a certain option or review some fundamental already taught, he just has to say, "Give me the Scramble Drill." The two units go to their designated baskets and the coach then just has to talk on what options he wants to teach or review. From this drill, I can tell just what option to work on. *Examples:*

1. Give me the shot in front of the double screen from WSW. Now give me the shot in front of double screen from SSW. Now hit either wing. The players have to move all through the pattern until they reach this option.

2. Hit the back track option after resetting by the SSW or WSW. *Note:* Add to the drill by putting a defensive man on each wing. The post can move all to either side. After wing resets he and the post learn to concentrate on picking this defensive man.

3. Give me rotation and strong side clear.

4. Give me the baseline pass from the SSW. *Note:* Add a defensive man on the post. As the drill is being run, he learns to hook this man and learns to shoot with a man "hacking" him. The man feeding learns to read the position of the defensive man. Naturally, a defensive man could be added to the SSW so that he learns to pass over the hand.

5. Run any part of the pattern but no shots except lay-ups to be taken. *Note:* No certain option is run and the players all learn to key their movement on the pass or the dribble that is made. In this type of drill, we are learning movement other than technique. Maybe the only shot to be taken is the lay-up by the cutter. In a 15-second period, a player is thrown in many spots in a short time. The players can reset, split, scramble into another basic working formation, rotate, and so on.

6. Give me the delay offense but only the overhead pass to the wing can result in a shot at the basket. *Note:* The coach can put a defense man only on the wing. In this way, the center learns to read the wing's defensive man. As we are learning movement, the center is also learning techniques of reading and picking.

The above are just a few examples. A defensive man can be added to defense against the option being run. As a coach is teaching a specific option he also is teaching movement. The slow part, and also the hard part, of teaching is doing the movement and then seeing the option that is being taught. As mentioned, each phase of teaching takes time: Drilling dummy, then with limited defense, half-court controlled, and the final step of full court.

The above Scramble Drill is used all year long. A coach has to decide what phase of the pattern seems weak and then just concentrate on that movement. All the coach has to say is to give me the Scramble Drill. The teams split as designated and then all the coach has to say is what phase of the pattern to work with. Naturally, at the beginning of the year, it is quite confusing but as the season progresses the better each phase of the pattern should be executed.

DOUBLE-SCREEN SHOOTING DRILL

We try to make many of our shooting drills fit the shooting spots where the shots will be taken. Many of our drills are where two or three men work together and I, as the coach, will say what shot I want them to work on. We will use the following drill all year to work just on this shot and movement. (See Diagram 138.)

1. 3 has the ball, 1 breaks hard into position, receives the ball from 3 and shoots.
2. Rebounder retrieves ball, dribbles out to 3 spot, 1 is next rebounder, 3 goes to 1's spot to be next shooter.

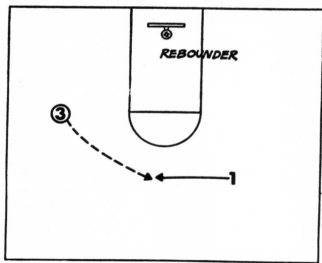

Diagram 138. Position for drill of Double Screen shot.

The drill takes time but each man has to learn to get himself set in position to shoot from this spot. Each day, time is spent on this drill because it is the same shot being taken in both zone and man-for-man offense. Naturally, we have to make the basic movement going to the right. If a gym has six baskets, then there is a group at each basket.

WEAK-SIDE-WING SHOOTING DRILL

This is another drill used all year. It gives all the wings a chance to work on their fundamental move of shooting and driving. (See Diagram 139.)

1. Ball at Point, P,—3 breaks out and pivots and shoots.
2. Rebounder retrieves the ball, dribbles to 3 spot, 3 goes to P, and P goes to rebounder.

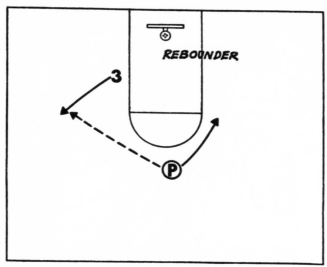

Diagram 139. Shows starting position for WSW shooting drill.

Coaching Points: 1. A coach can tell the group what shot to take: Drive baseline for shot, drive at middle and pull up to shoot, just turn and shoot, and so on. In other words, practice each day on different moves and shots by the WSW. Naturally, this has to be done on both the right and left side. 2. Make P move away from 3, just as in the regular pattern, then take the rebounding spot. 3. If a coach wants to, he can have the rebounder be a defensive man on 3. 4. Have as many groups working as there are baskets.

LAY–UP AND DRIBBLING DRILL

Lay-ups should be practiced all year at all levels: College, high school, and junior high.

1. There should be two groups, each going to its basket.
2. Ideal if each boy has a ball.
3. 1 dribbles in, shoots lay-up, retrieves own ball, and dribbles back to his own line; as 1 dribbles back, 2 dribbles in, etc.
4. Four types of shots are: Right-handed lay-up, underneath lay-up, reverse turn and jump shot, and reverse turn at center of court and come at the basket straight on.

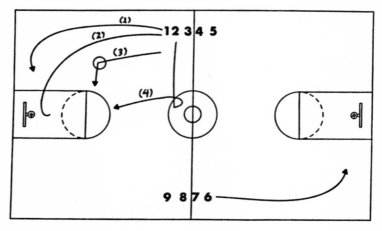

Diagram 140. Lay-up and Dribbling Drill.

5. Each line executes right-handed and then reverses around and then has to shoot left-handed.

6. Daily drill, go through it three times; takes about eight to nine minutes.

7. Teaches different lay-ups, dribbling, and reverse turns.

8. As the player is dribbling back to the line from the basket, he works dribbling with the left hand.

3-ON-2 FAST-BREAK DRILL

1. 5, 6, 7 break against 3, 4.

2. Once 3, 4 secure ball, the 3, 4, and 10 break against 1 and 2.

3. Two men of the 5, 6, and 7 group have to stay on defense and other man goes to end of line.

4. Now 1, 2, and 8 break.

5. The drill teaches Tandem defensing against break and all the principles that a coach wishes to teach 3-on-2.

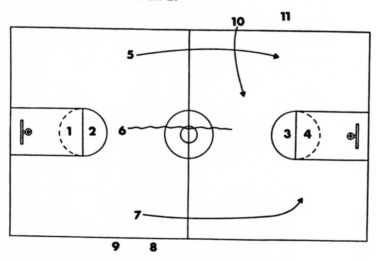

Diagram 141. 3-on-2 Fast Break Drill.

6. The drill gives each man a chance on defense and also gives each man a chance on handling the break.
7. Once drill is taught seven to eight minutes, three times a week, it gives the team a continuous review of the break principles.

3-ON-3 DRILL, FULL COURT

1. 1, 2, and 3 on defense against 4, 5, and 6.
2. Pressure ball in bounds.
3. Once ball is inbounds 4, 5, and 6 try to score. If shot is taken, and rebound secured by 1, 2, or 3, then they try to fast-break and try to score on 4, 5, and 6.

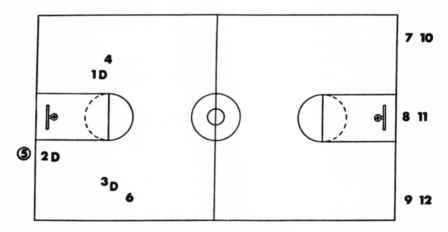

Diagram 142. 3-on-3 Drill Full Court.

4. If 4, 5, and 6 score, the 1, 2, and 3 go against 7, 8, and 9.
5. The drill teaches many things:

    A. Bringing the ball up the court under pressure.
    B. Learning to get the ball inbounds under pressure.
    C. Defensive principles the coach wishes to teach.

D.   Reaction to fast-break both offensively and defensively.
E.   Gives the players a chance to free-lance and work on offensive fundamentals.

ONE-ON-ONE DEFENSIVE DRILL, FULL COURT

1.   Groups work in pairs.
2.   7 tries to advance ball up the court against 10, 2 tries to advance ball up court against 1.
3.   Each group has half court to work in.
4.   When group finishes, go to end of line and then, when turn comes up, other man in pair brings the ball up the court.
5.   Drill teaches dribbling under pressure, dribbler learns to use reverse turns, change of pace, behind the back, and so forth. Each man will develop his own technique.
6.   Good conditioner for man on defense. Should learn to stop dribbler, guide, overplay, etc.
7.   Drill time is seven to eight minutes. Can be used all season.
8.   Drill makes all players work on defensive and offensive fundamentals.

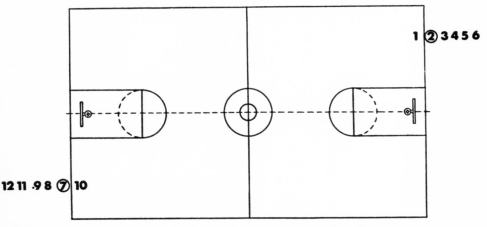

Diagram 143. One-on-One Defensive Drill Full Court.

Denying and Defense 9

There are many and various ways to play defense in basketball. There are many ways to approach defensive basketball. There is one way we can approach defense and that is to say—that defense is denial. For everything that we attempt to do offensively, the defense is doing the opposite—denying what we are attempting to do—score or getting the ball in position to score.

Each coach will develop his own philosophy on how to stop the other team from scoring or it may be looked at the other way—how to outscore the other team. A team might try to outscore the other team by running and trying to shoot more than the other club, or it might try to run such a pattern that it tries to work the ball in closer than the other team by taking a better percentage shot; or then, again, it might try to concentrate and make the defense so strong that it really complements its offense by denying the other club its offense—and in this way its offense does not have the big burden to score so many points.

The denial in any coach's teaching will be limited to his personnel. If a basketball player is not quick, then his denial ability will be limited in his individual defense and in his help-denial team defense. A coach may know his defense, and teach it, but he will be limited in his success in denial defense by the quickness of his personnel. Defensive technique can be taught but then will have its limitations because of the speed, or lack of it, of the ball players.

Team denial defenses can take many shapes or forms. These defenses might be full-court zone traps, half-court traps, full-court, man-for-man pressure, half-court, man-for-man, collapsing zones, collapsing man-for-man defense, or combination defenses. Some defenses will deny the pass inbounds or try to deny the dribbler to advance the ball, deny all passing lanes, deny the cutters to take certain tracks, or may only deny passes into the lane and not deny any perimeter passes. Each coach has to try to decide on the type of denial defense that he wishes his team to use. His defenses will be limited to his personnel and will be changed with the situations in the ball games, depending on whether you are ahead, or behind, on the score.

Time is a factor to any coach in his teaching. There is a limit to how many things a coach can teach his club on offense and defense. There are limitations because of time and also limitations due to ability of his ball players. The basic defense the coach teaches should be sound because it will meet many various types of offenses.

Basketball is a percentage game. If two teams are equal, then the team that takes the best percentage shot should win. This good percentage shot has to be developed from the team's offensive movement. The philosophy can also be looked at defensively—if the team's defense can give a lower percentage shot at the basket than its own offense gets, then it should win.

There are many denial defensives that a coach can use in building his defensive philosophy. In building this defense, the fundamental principles have to be sound to meet many types of offensive movements.

THE BALL SHOULD NOT BE DRIBBLED BETWEEN TWO DEFENSIVE PLAYERS

No matter what type of defense a team uses, it usually will have this one principle involved and that is to keep the ball out of this area as shown in Diagram 144. The only time the ball should get in this area is when it is shot. This principle is impossible to accomplish but this is what denial defense is trying to do—each time the other club has the ball. If the defense can keep the team from dribbling or passing into the area, then the shots will come from outside this area.

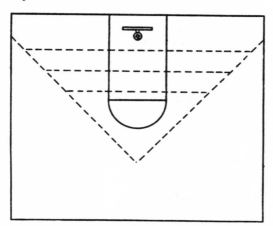

Diagram 144. No penetration area.

A fundamental defensive denial principle is that the ball should not be dribbled between two defensive players or between a defensive player and the baseline. If this principle is adhered to, then it's hard to penetrate into the scoring area or penetrate closer to the basket. To execute this principle, a coach has to teach help-denying defense. The speed and quickness of defensive players helps in teaching this one ingredient fundamental. As a general rule, one player can't keep another player from advancing the ball and this is where and how each player helps in building a team defense. A few examples of this principle are explained below.

1. The ball is passed into the post and he pivots into the middle for his shot. Odds are that he moved between the defensive post man and a defensive man on the outside. The offensive post man thus moved between two defensive players. It is better percentage for the defense if the ball has to be moved out for the shot than if the post shoots from inside.

2. The offensive man tries to drive the baseline, but the defensive man shuts him off. The driver executes a reverse, turns, and goes in for the basket. Odds are he went between two defensive players. (See Diagram 145.) The defensive player off the ball, X2, made the mistake of allowing a man to dribble between him and another defensive man. The X2

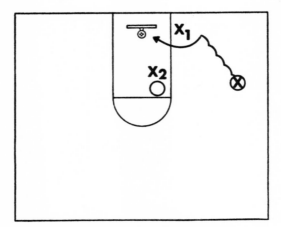

Diagram 145. Ball dribbled between two defensive men.

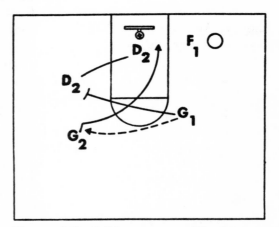

Diagram 146. Ball between two defensive men.

man should move into the path of the dribbler. Too many times players will reach in and not move in.

3. Offensive G1 passes to G2, he blocks and G2 goes down the middle, but while going to the basket he goes inside F1. (See Diagram 146.) F1 has made the mistake of allowing G2 to dribble between himself and defensive D2. F1 should not reach in to stop the dribbler but should move in physically to stop the ball. F1 still is responsible for his offensive man if the ball is passed to him. He has to hit and recover.

DEFENSE—LINE OF FLIGHT

The principle that has to be presented when teaching help off the ball is the defensive player and the line of flight between himself, his man, and the ball. The line of flight is defined as the line from the ball to any other offensive man. (See Diagram 147.) There are a number of defensive principles that are taught in relationship to the line of flight. A defensive player can play three places in relationship to this line—behind it, on it, or in front of it. The defensive players 1 and 4, as shown in Diagram 147, might be playing on or in front of the line of flight and denying the pass to either player, but the defensive man on 3 should be playing behind it. This 3 man should have his back to the basket, feet perpendicular to the line of flight. In this position, he can always see his man and the ball. He is the man in our help-denying defense to help on the post man who is being pressured by the number 2 defensive man. The farther the offensive man is from the ball, the farther the defensive man can play from his offensive man.

Every time the ball is passed or is dribbled, every man should be moving because the line of flight is changed. With just a short pass or a dribble, each defense man goes from a denying man to help-denying man. *Example:* Ball is moved from 5 to 4

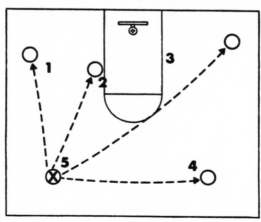

Diagram 147. Line of flight.

in Diagram 147; now 3 becomes a denial man while 1 drops off from the line of flight. This fundamental has to be repeated— "Every time the ball moves, every defensive man should move."

DEFENSE AND THE POST

In denying the ball to a post man, there are three post positions a team has to defend: High post, medium post, and low post. (See Diagram 148.) A man in the low post area should always be fronted and the pass denied to this offensive man. Many teams will run guards or forwards into this area and if the man is successful in getting the ball in this area, he will usually score.

The defensive man on the high post should play the ball side of the post. It is dangerous to front this man because back-side help might not be available. If the ball is passed to the high post man, the defensive man must now back off him. This allows cutters to slide through and not being close to the post man allows the offensive man to make his first move to free himself for the shot. The man is not a threat as long as his back is to the basket. Once he pivots and faces the basket, the defensive man tightens up and plays him tough.

The medium post man is a hard spot to deny the basketball. A coach may always try to front this man and then

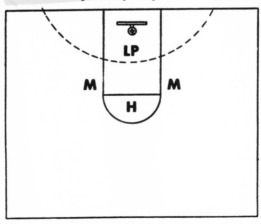

Diagram 148. Shows three post positions.

hope for back-side help from another defensive player. A man that can help on this pass is the defensive man on the ball. If pressure is applied on the man trying to make the pass in, then the offensive player has a much harder time making a good accurate pass. A general rule for playing the medium post and denying the pass is to play on the ball side of the post. If the ball is above the free-throw line, then the defensive post should be on the high side and if the ball is lower than the free-throw line the defensive man should be on the low side. If the ball is moving from above the free-throw line to lower free-throw line, the post man must also move. To keep denying the post man the ball the defensive man at this point should front the post, keep his eye on the ball, and work himself around to the baseline side.

DEFENSE AND THE SCREEN

Two defensive denying fundamentals that are hard work are denying the pass and denying the dribbler to use a stationary screen to free himself. The best way of denying the dribbler the use of the screen is for the defense man to go to the top of the screen. The defense man on the dribbler has to be warned about the screen. This is the job of the man who is guarding the screener. The defensive men have to learn to straighten up as they come into the screen. If the man is alerted and he can learn to straighten up, then he has a good chance of getting over the top of the screen with the dribbler.

No matter how hard a player works to get over the top of screens, there will be times when the defense doesn't accomplish this. The next best thing for the defense to do is for the defensive man on the screener to open up and let the other defensive man slide through. This doesn't prevent the shot over the screen but it does allow the defensive man to pick up the dribbler as he comes over the screen. The defense man on the dribbler should never allow two men, screener and defensive man, between him and the ball. If this happens, then the dribbler has penetrated too far before the defense man can recover or turn him. Screens will be successful and the defense has to be prepared to handle this situation. The defense tries to get over the top, but runs into the screener. A shift has to be made and this should be an aggressive one. The man taking the dribbler should flatten out the dribbler and not allow him to turn the corner, forcing him to the side line. If he pulls up to pass off, then this aggressiveness should help on defensing an accurate pass to the screen who might be rolling to the basket. The defensive man who was screened must fight himself to the ball side and take the screener who is rolling to the basketball. Along with denying the pass into the scoring area, the team also has to deny the dribbler the use of the screener. Defense is hard work plus team defensive execution. This defensive execution includes use of the voice, straightening up, opening up, sliding over or through, aggressive shifting, and then denying the pass to the screener who is rolling to the basket.

FAST BREAK AND DENIAL

A defensive problem for any team is trying to contain a fast-break basketball team. No team can break without the ball, so the best denial defense is to try to control the basketball offensively. The better percentage shot that a team takes, the less chance for the fast-breaking team to break from a rebound. If a team can control the ball for a good percentage shot and not turn the ball over, then it is denying the other team from fast-breaking. The Shuffle Offense is a good denying offense. It is a controlled offense that can be, and is, geared to go for just the high percentage shot. No matter what offense is used, if the coach can discipline his club for the high percentage shot, then theoretically the team is using denying defense—denying the team from its fast-break offense.

Fast-break basketball is reaction basketball—reacting from defense to offense. The fast-breaking team that can react, release, and execute is a problem for any team. The reaction is also in reverse. A ball player must also react from offense to defense. A shot is taken and the ball secured with a rebound. As soon as that ball was rebounded and secured by the defense, then the other team now must react. The player was on offense;

now, immediately, he is playing defense. The first denial of the fast-break is to stop the outlet pass. Why did the player not get the rebound? He was blocked out by the player who did get the rebound. Now, he must react and not let the outlet pass be made.

The second man who has to react to the break is the defense man opposite the lane where the outlet pass is to be made to. This is the man to try to fill the third lane on the break. The man who also has to react is the offensive man who was on that side for the rebound. He must also react to get back on defense as quickly as possible when he sees the ball rebounded on the opposite side.

The third denying phase of trying to stop the break is to try to help the man who received the out pass from penetrating. The pass will at times be successful, but if this man can be kept from penetrating into the offensive end of the court, then the break will be slowed down.

The fast-breaking team is successful in filling up the three lanes and it has outnumbered the defense 3 to 2. The defense first must deny the team the lay-up shot—it must protect the basket. The ball must be challenged to attempt to delay its penetration as long as possible, hoping to get a third man down on the defense. One of the ways of defensing 3-on-2 is the tandem method as shown in Diagram 149. 1 challenges A who

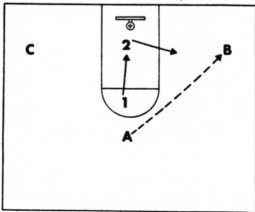

Diagram 149. Movement on tandem fastbreak.

passes to B; now 2 takes B and 1 drops back to protect the basket. If B passes back to A, 2 takes the ball and now the defense is back in its tandem defense. By this time, help should be forthcoming.

DENIAL AND THE SHUFFLE

The Shuffle is a very controlled offense and players must get to certain spots to execute it properly. Denying the offense these certain spots makes it hard for the players to execute. One denying pass is the pass to the Shuffle Cutter. (See Diagram 150.) The D man on the Shuffle Cutter should go over the top of the screen set by the post. He should take his eye off the ball and concentrate his efforts on just the cutter. As the cutter comes off the screen, he should work hard to stay between the ball and the offense man. If the cutter comes to the low post position, he should front this position.

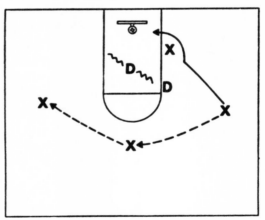

Diagram 150. Defense shuffle cut.

Another denial pass is the pass to the weak-side wing who is trying to get into position to feed the cutter. If this pass is controlled, then the offense has to go to its secondary part of the offense. If the pass is contested but completed, the timing will be off between the cutter and the passer. The offense team will work hard on the back-door pass, but the one man in the help position for this pass is the defensive man on the post. If the pass is made down the lane, this defensive man on the post should be ready for the interception.

A third denying spot is the overplaying of the point man. This forces the offense, or rather the strong-side forward, to go to a secondary option and denies the offense from getting into its shuffle cut. If the offense is not prepared for this pressure, then it creates problems in getting its movement started properly.

Another type of denial encountered to stop the shuffle cut is to pressure the weak-side forward and then sag. The pass might be made, but by the pressure, if it is completed, is made out farther than normal. Once the pass is completed, the defense sags and this then makes it hard to pass to the cutter. This also forces the offense into a secondary part of its movement by sagging.

OTHER DENYING PRINCIPLES

A player who has dribbled must be played and respected for his drive. A good, smart defensive player will learn the capabilities of the offensive player as to his driving and use of the dribble. If an offensive man is strongly right-handed, then the defense should deny him or try to restrict his dribbling with the right hand and force the offensive man to use his off hand. Any time a dribbler picks up his dribble, each defensive man should try to restrict or prevent a pass to his man. The man on the dribbler, especially, should try to over-pressure to force a bad pass. Here again defense is alertness and reaction—playing the dribbler and reacting to force the bad pass.

The offensive team has the ball out of bounds under its own basket. The defense has penetrated into the scoring area and defense should try to force the ball to the outside. Many teams will play zone in this situation in order to try to protect against out-of-bounds plays. If a team stays in its man-for-man defense, then the player on the ball should help protect the basket area for a throw-in. (See Diagram 151.) By playing in position B, the defense does protect the pass-in toward the basket.

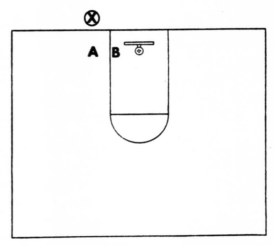

Diagram 151. Defense out of bounds.

REVIEW

The denying defense is successful if execution is good. Execution on defense is just as important as it is on offense. If one man fails to execute properly, then the defense breaks down. If execution is a failure due to lack of hustle, then this really hurts the total defensive picture. Some ball players will execute better than others because of speed and quickness. The desire to play denial defense is the unknown factor. Each time the other club gets possession of the basketball, this desire, along with the execution, is a must if the team defense is to be a good one.

Denial defense or any type of defense can be summed up this way: "Never give an opponent the shot or move he likes best." The defensive player should keep pressure on the offensive player with the ball at all times when he is within scoring distance. Denial defense then is denying the passing lanes, denying the dribbler to advance the ball, and above all, denying a player and the opponent the percentage shot. If by offense execution the offense team can get a better shot at the basket, and denies the other team its percentage shot, then the team should have a winner.

TRAP—DENYING—DEFENSE

There are many and various types of zones and traps, half-court, full-court, combination and match-up zones. A coach can't teach all of them so he has to decide what defense fits into his philosophy and also fits his personnel. The traps and zones are basically used for various reasons:

1. Control the tempo of the game. If by its use of a trap or zone, a team can control and speed the tempo of the game to fit into the coach's need, then it has accomplished its purpose. The team that can play its type of game, slow or fast, will have a good chance of winning. A team that is slow and deliberate and doesn't want to run, and can continue to slow the game up controls the tempo to its advantage. But if this slow and deliberate team can be speeded up by the use of zones and traps, then the tempo is controlled by the opponent. The reverse also works—if the pattern ball club can slow up the breaking team, then it also has accomplished its purpose. It is much harder to be deliberate and slow the game to its tempo because the traps and zones force the opposing team to the tempo of the pattern team.

Throughout the years of watching games, I have observed many times the tempo changed by the use of zones. The tempo also works in reverse. The team is running and executing well against man-for-man defense and then by a change to a zone defense the tempo is slowed down. The tempo gets the team standing because of the change so it does work in reverse.

2. Stop a pattern ball club. A well-disciplined pattern ball club has to spend many practice hours working on its movement and techniques so one way to combat and control this movement is through the use of zones and traps. This forces the team to use its zone offense, which might not be as intricate.

3. The blocking game can also be controlled by the use of zones and traps.

4. The zone is conducive to less fouling, and also, a man in foul trouble can be helped on defense much more in the zone than man-for-man.

A combination zone and trap defense that combines with our man-for-man principles is the 1-2-1-1. The alignment is shown in Diagram 152. Just as in man-for-man, the defense is trying to keep the ball out of the good scoring area as shown in the diagram. Theoretically speaking, if a team can get a better shot and the same number of shots at the basket than the

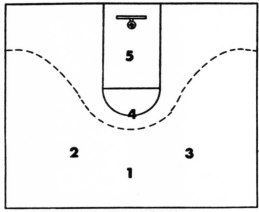

Diagram 152. Shows denying area, trap alignment.

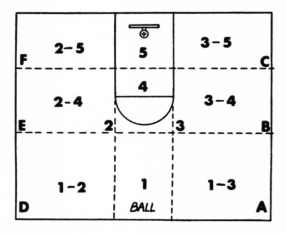

Diagram 153. General zone trap responsibility.

opponent, it should win. The approximate areas of responsibility are shown in Diagram 153.

If the ball is guided into area A as shown in Diagram 153, then 1 and 3 trap. The movement and responsibility to them will be as shown in Diagram 154. Rules for movement and area now are:

> 2—high post and reversal pass.
> 4—high post and wing area.
> 5—back side and long pass into C area.

Ball is moved into area B, movement and rules now are:

> 2—drops, responsible for back side.
> 4—takes ball in his area.
> 3—drops to ball and tries to trap with B.
> 1—drops to free throw circle—responsible for pass into high or medium post.
> 5—plays medium post on baseline side—fronts low post.

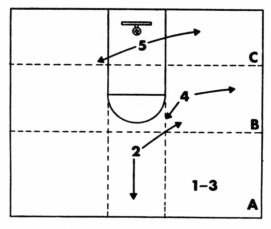

Diagram 154. Responsibility—Ball in Area A.

To keep from penetrating, a defensive principle involved is that the ball should not be dribbled between two defensive ball players. As 3 drops to help 4, this is his big responsibility.

No shot developed for wing and ball moves to the corner. Our areas of responsibility and rules are:

> 5—takes ball; defensive rule, protect baseline.
> 4—drops, fronts low post man.
> 3—drops to ball, once again helps on trap, doesn't let ball be penetrated by dribbling between him and 5.
> 2—back side.
> 1—falls and tries to prevent pass to medium post.

If the ball was forced to area D instead of area A, then 1 and 2 would trap and the same rules and movement described above would prevail to the left side.

A team makes the first pass after trap back to the middle of the court instead of to the wing. Now the rules and movement are as shown in Diagram 155.

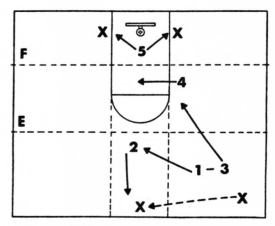

Diagram 155. Movement on reversal pass.

> 2—plays ball; tries to force the pass into area E and F wide and high.
> 1—must recover to middle of court, gets between ball and basket.
> 5—responsible for any pass to low post men in his area as designated by an X on the diagram.

The men should now be approximately in their positions as shown in Diagram 156.

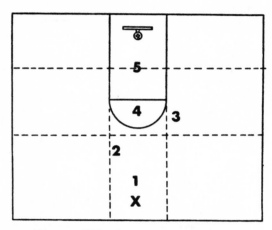

**Diagram 156. Approximate position—
ball in center of court.**

If the ball is moved to area E, our rules prevail as discussed: 4 and 2 take the ball, 1 falls to medium and high post area, 3 has back side, and 5 now covers medium post on baseline side.

Instead of assigning areas to cover, a team can try to trap from its position on the court when pressuring man for man. (See Diagram 157.)

Example: As G_1 is pressuring and forces guard into area A, each player reacts to the pressure G_1 is maintaining. F_5 turns his man loose and helps trap with G_1; C_4 is alerted and ready to intercept pass to F_5; G_2 should have turned his man loose and stays in the center of the court. In other words, the players assume the number and assignments as discussed in Diagram 154.

G_1 —becomes 1.
F_5 —becomes 3.
G_2 —becomes the 2 man.
G_4 —becomes 4.
G_3 —becomes 5.

Once the players become these numbers, they stay with them until a shot is taken or the ball is turned over, or the team gets the ball out of bounds.

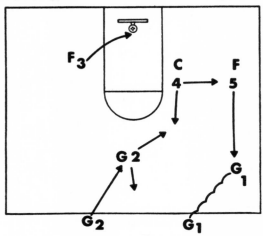

Diagram 157. Movement, trap by F and G.

Another way of trapping is shown in Diagram 158, which illustrates the two guards trapping in area A. (If this happens, then G_1 would become 3, G_2 become 1, F_3 become 2, 4 stay 4, and F_5 become 5.)

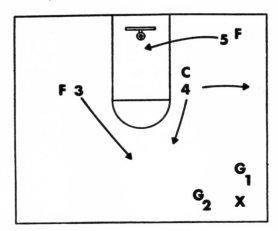

Diagram 158. Movement, guards trapping.

In this manner of trapping, the trap is disguised and it keeps the offensive team guessing, but it takes a lot of practice for the defensive players to react to, and execute, the trap situations. One time down the court, a guard might be the point or 1 man and the next time the 2 or 3 man. This also changes the forwards' duties. The forward may be the 5 man once and next time the 3 or 2 man. In this trapping, the players have to team more than one position and can't specialize in positions.

In reviewing the trap, many of the same defensive principles are taught as in man-for-man:

1. Keep the ball out of percentage shooting area.
2. Keep the offensive from penetrating by not letting a player drive the baseline or between two defensive players.
3. Every time the ball moves, every defensive man must move.
4. Keep pressure on the man with the ball.
5. Front low post and try to keep ball away from medium and high post.

1 - 4 and the Shuffle 10

Another formation that a team can use on entering in the BWF instead of the two-man front is the one-man front. The 1-4 formation is very adaptable as another entry into our shuffle offense instead of the Tandem formations as discussed in Chapter 1. The 1-4 gives the team another maneuverable and different way of basically getting into our shuffle offense and BWF. Diagram 159 shows the 1-4 formation.

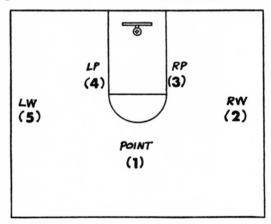

Diagram 159. 1-4 Formation.

The numbers and men shown in Diagram 159 will be referred to throughout the chapter. A coach can specialize as to positions each player has to run or, if the team and players are adaptable, they may start and run all different spots. The height of the positions of the players on the court depends upon the pressure the team receives when entering its BWF.

As explained in Chapter 1, the BWF has to be established before the shuffle movement can be started. The Ten and Twenty Series are both used to establish it. One advantage of the 1-4 is that a team can easily enter either the right or left wing to establish the BWF. For some reason, the point might be told to enter on a certain side but either wing can very easily be entered.

If the point starts his movement at the right wing, then this man attempts to receive the ball in the same spot as the No. 2 man in our Tandem formation. The position is shown in Diagram 160. He should try to receive the ball in a straight line with the RP and the basket. To establish our BWF, the point goes to the corner.

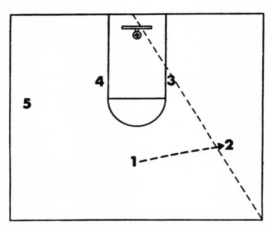

**Diagram 160. Shows where RW
should receive ball.**

If the defense pressures this pass, then the next look for the point man is to try to hit the RP. The RP's first move is to look for the back door pass to the RW who breaks to the basket just as soon as he sees that he is overplayed and can't receive the ball. A well-executed pass by the point is to skip the RP and hit the RW going to the basket. (See Diagram 161.) If the post is hit, he tries to hit the RW; as he is looking in, the point takes his man in and he tries to rub his man on the post for the second option of the post. If no shots develop, the players have to scramble into their BWF. The post could dribble to the 2 spot, point to corner, and RW to the No. 3 spot.

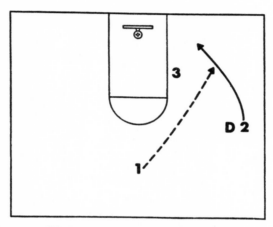

Diagram 161. Back door to R.W.

Once the BWF is established the No. 2 man has the same options in the 1-4 as in our Tandem Formations.

    1.   Hit the post and split. Same split rules prevail.
    2.   Hit the corner. Here again we can split or rotate.
    3.   Hit the point.

As soon as the RW is hit the LW takes his man in and he can come to the point or the LP can bounce out to the point and the LW becomes the LP. This movement depends upon the personnel or who the coach wishes to be at the LP spot. As the LW comes out and is being pressured, he comes straight out and the LP pops out for the blind pig. This same movement was discussed in Chapter 2.

The point can move the ball to either wing and they in turn have the same options the wings had, as discussed in Chapter 2. The LW has the options:

1. Turn and face the basket, drive or shoot.
2. Hit the cutter or post.
3. Double screen.
4. Reset.

If the point moves the ball to the man who comes to the strong-side wing then he has the options:

1. Turn, look at the basket, drive or hit the post with the baseline pass.
2. Post moves up, hit him, and then split.
3. Double screen.
4. Reset.

So the big and only difference in the 1-4 and the Tandem is the entry into the BWF.

TWENTY SERIES

The Twenty Series can be very easily used. The point just dribbles to the RW's or LW's position and waves that wing to the corner. Now, the same options can be run by the guard as the wing. A coach can very easily tell the team to situation Twenty Series. *Example:* On all baskets made you enter into BWF by the Twenty Series.

USE OF PERSONNEL

If a coach has only one good center and always wants to key this man on the post, he can very easily do this. The easiest way is to tell the point man to enter on the post's side. He can tell the post always to be on a certain side and then enter on this side, or the point has to look to see where the post man is and then enter on that side. The question that comes up at this time is: What if the point can't enter on that side? This situation can easily be solved. If the point enters away from the good post, No. 4 in Diagram 162, the following movement would then take place: RP to corner, LW to point, point to LP, and No. 4 breaks to RP's spot. This, then, keeps the good post and his proper position. As in the Tandem formations, the players in the 1-4 also have to be able to run all spots.

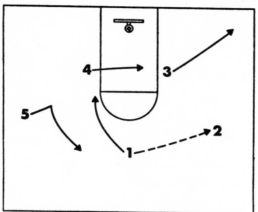

**Diagram 162   Shows movement
if entry is away from post.**

The team has two men who can handle themselves equally well on the post. This also creates problems for the defense. The problem that is created defensively is a forward, not too proficient as a defensive post man, has to be on the post. Now, to create the mismatch the point must try to enter on the side away from the big post. The pass that is tried now is the baseline pass by the strong-side wing and if this is not successful, the ball is returned back to the point and then back to the original strong side, and the baseline pass once again is tried. A good technique to take the big man away from his spot is to break out the post to the point spot. This takes the big man away from the defensive board and helps take the pressure of reserving the ball from a wing to the point.

In the 1-4, the post does pop to the point position many times. (See Diagram 163 for movement.) A small change in rule is made in our double-screen situation. The rule for the point, as mentioned in Chapter 2, is when passing to a wing to go away from the ball. (See Diagram 164.) In Diagram 164, No. 4 can move the ball to either wing 5 or 1 breaking to their positions.

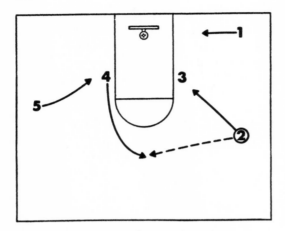

Diagram 163. Post to the point.

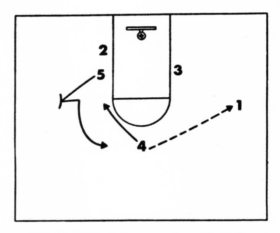

Diagram 164. Point away from the ball.

Example: 4 moves ball to 1—back to original strong side. As mentioned, his rule is to go away from ball. (See Diagram 164.) The change in movement is this—as 5 is coming to double-screen situation, 4 continues down the lane and blocks on No. 2's man. Remember No. 2 was the cutter and sets opposite the post. The situation is now as shown in Diagram 165. 5 can now shoot or hit No. 2 low who should be free because of the block by No. 4. This is just a small change in the double-screen situation that can be worked if the big man comes away from the post spot. This same situation develops if No. 4 moves the ball to the No. 5 man, weak-side forward. (See Diagram 166.)

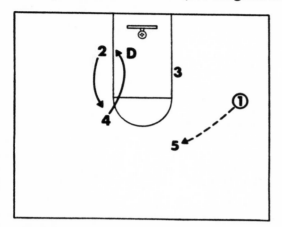

Diagram 165. Post blocks low away from ball.

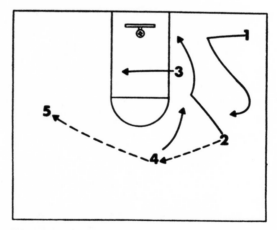

Diagram 166. Shows movement post hits WSW.

First, No. 5 looks for his options as the WSW: drive, hit the cutter or post, or go into the double-screen situation. If the double screen is run, then 4, who has gone away from the ball, continues down the free throw lane line and blocks on No. 2's man. Remember the cutter sets opposite the post. (See Diagram 167.) If 1 does not shoot, he may move the ball over to No. 2 coming off the screen set by 4. After No. 1 passes, he goes down the lane and 5 comes out. Now No. 2 controls the play—shoot, hit 4 inside, or still hit 5 coming up in front of the post.

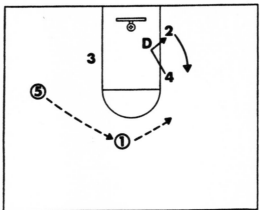

Diagram 167. Post blocks low on double screen.

This situation can always be run by all personnel and not just with the big man, but it does take away the big man handling the ball and it places him in a very good low post position to rebound and also in a good position to receive the ball inside from the man he blocked for who is always the cutter.

SPECIAL SITUATIONS

Many of the special situations and plays discussed in Chapter 5 can be run from the 1-4 formations. If a situation is to be designated as to a side, a coach just has to call out right side or left side. He can very easily designate the series Ten or Twenty.

Example of special play: The coach wishes to clear the floor for some individual on a free throw missed. He may say, run Twenty Series to the right. The club sets up its formation and then the point will dribble to the RW spot and the RW will start to clear out as the point dribbles to him. (See Diagram 168.) The clear situation can be set up for either LW or LP. This can be decided in advance as to who is going to run the clear as discussed in Chapter 5.

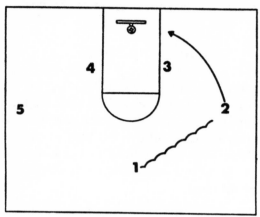

Diagram 168. 20 series right, clear.

The point man is the good shooter and also has to bring the ball up the court to set the offense. A situation that can be run for this man is the baseline pick for the corner man. The

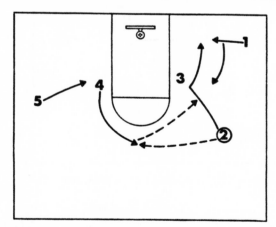

Diagram 169. Baseline pick for the point.

coach can say on all baskets made, run the baseline pick for the corner. The point can enter and set up the BWF on either the right or left side. The series should be Ten, in this way the point man will be in the corner. (See Diagram 169.) Now either LW or LP can break for the pass from RW. The RW picks for the point who receives the ball for the shot in front of the post.

1-4 AND THE ZONE

The 1-4 attack against the zone is very similar in its basic movements as discussed in Chapter 6. The basic alignment is the same as shown in Diagram 159. The point can make the entry pass to either wing. He then follows his pass so that he is even with the free throw line extended. The team should now be approximately in the alignment as shown in Diagram 170. The RW2 now has the options:

1. Shooting, driving the baseline and shooting.
2. Hit the RP3 who slides down into the low post position.

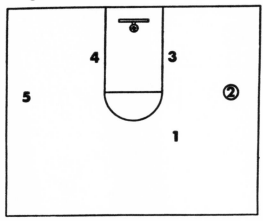

Diagram 170. Alignment when RW₂ has ball.

He may hit the post immediately or he can hit him after driving toward the baseline and then looking in again. Sometimes, the 3 man will pause as he slides down and other times he will continue moving under the basket to a low post position on the left side and the LP4 will rotate into the right post's position. He also is a target for the 2 man. Each defense will play this movement differently and what options open will vary in each game and with each entry.

Option 3 for the RW2 is to move the ball back to the point. Now the P1 may shoot. The board is well covered by 3, 4, and 2 who goes to the baseline after passing to P1. The 1 man will look for the low post man 3. Other than shooting, the main passing option is to the LW5 who has moved up and even with the 1 man. (See Diagram 171.) The position of 5 will vary to the defense being played. More shots will be taken at this spot than any other position. The board is well covered by 3, 4, 2, and 1 as the out rebounder inside the lane.

If a shot does not develop for the 5 man, the following movement takes place and this develops the following option for 5. (See Diagram 172.) The 3 man blocks on the baseline for 2 who went along the baseline as soon as he passed to 1. What happens on this block again varies with the defense.

If 2 receives the pass, his options now are to shoot, look inside for the 3 man or look for 4 breaking into a high post position along the lane with 3. If 4 is hit high, he shoots, looks for 3 inside, or looks for 1 on the opposite side. After 1 passed to 5, he should have moved down low for back-side rebounding

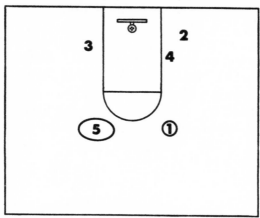

Diagram 171. Alignment when 1 is
ready to move ball to 5.

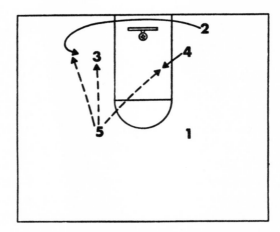

Diagram 172. Passing options for 5.

position. If no shots develop from this movement, the team has to reset into its basic 1-4 formation and start its movement once again.

The team has the same movement if the point 1 enters the 1-4 on the left side to the LW5. Now 5 can shoot, drive, hit the LP, or move the ball back to the point who has followed his pass so he is even with the free-throw line. The team should be in the same position as shown in Diagram 170 except it is now on the left side. The movement and options would now be the same if the entry was made on the right side.

With the above movement, the zone offense creates many good shots around the key and down on the baseline. The board is usually covered by the two big men inside along the lane. The placement of personnel in the zone is such that the ball handlers and good outside shooters should be at the wing spots and at the point. The movement is adaptable to many types of zones. Just as in any offense, the players must recognize, and make, the openings for their shots.

Diamond and Monster Defense   11

Another type of zone-trap defense is the diamond and monster.[1] It adheres to, and uses, many of the man-for-man denying principles that have been discussed in Chapter 10. The basic perimeter defense tries to deny any shots into the area outlined in Diagram 173.

If a team can be denied shots in this area, by getting shots from their offense into this area, then, theoretically, a team should win because of a better percentage shot.

The approximate areas of responsibility are shown in Diagram 173. Note that the monster is not included in this responsibility. When the offensive man has the ball in any of these areas, he is played tough and pressured man-for-man.

The diamond and monster has basic rules for, and can be used in, these defenses:

    A.   Basic perimeter.
    B.   Pressure.
    C.   Trap.

The rules for each of the above defenses will be described as to how they fit into what is known as the diamond and monster.

The placement of the personnel in the diamond and monster should be:

Point: Smallest guard.

Wings: Post man and biggest forward. These two men will be

---

[1] Monster name and idea from *Tempo Control Basketball*, Harry L. "Mike" Harkins, West Nyack, N.Y.: Parker Publishing Company, Inc., 1970.

in rebounding areas most often. They also will be the men who will get to the vulnerable trap area.

Base: Quickest and smallest forward. He has a lot of area to cover.

Monster: Biggest guard or best defensive "head." This man has to read situations and must adapt to different situations that occur within the game.

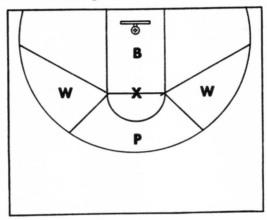

Diagram 173. Basic Coverage Area.
X—Basic Spot.

BASIC PERIMETER

The general rules for each man in the diamond and monster in our basic perimeter are:

Point: Stay between ball and basic spot (X) shown in diagram. Reason: This always keeps him in position to keep the ball out of the high post position.

W-Ball Side: Pressure man with the ball if he is in your area. Help prevent pass to low post area if guard has ball out in front-even with the free-throw lane extended.

W-Back Side: Stay approximately eight feet away from base man. When ball is in far corner, this will place him in position in front of low post.

Base: Guards man with ball from corner to corner. Ball in wing area, prevent pass to low and medium post.

General Rule for Point—Wings—Base: These four men should

always take the form of a diamond and pressure any man with the ball in their area. If a man tries to dribble out of your area, stay with him until a shift is made with one of the other diamond men.

Monster: General rule is back-side rebound. His special movement and rules will be discussed later.

The perimeter-diamond-monster defense is and can be disguised to make itself look like man for man defense. The

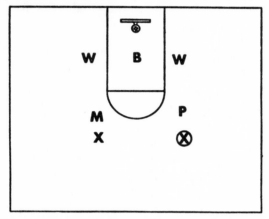

Diagram 174. Shows defense two-man front.

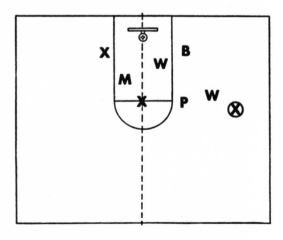

Diagram 175. Ball in Wing area.

guards can be pushed full court or half court. A general rule is
to try to push the ball by the point man. This puts the monster
on the guard without the ball. *Example:* The ball is worked
down the floor in the following position as shown in Diagram
174. The entry pass is made into the near wing's area. The
movement then would be as shown in Diagram 175. *Note rules:*
Ball wing pressure basketball; Base help low and medium post;
Back wing eight feet for B, P between ball and basic spot, note
diamond alignment; Monster back side. Now special rules for
monster:

1.   When ball is in wing area, he is responsible for
      offensive man in low spot X as shown in
      diagram.

Ball is moved into corner, now the movement is shown in
Diagram 176.

Rules: Base-pressure basketball: No one drives baseline; Back
W, front low post; Point, between post and basic spot; Ball W,
pressure reversal pass—might occasionally trap. Note diamond
alignment. Monster splits two X men. Tries to prevent long pass
to either man.

Special Monster Rules: If reversal pass is made from a
wing area to the front guard as shown in Diagram 177, monster
tries to move up quickly to pressure shot, but also tries to shut
off lane to X1. Remember, wing men are responsible for pass
into low post area when the ball is with a guard who is even
with the free-throw lane extended, but this wing might be late
getting over into position.

Any time there is a two-man front as shown in the
diagram, the monster helps with penetration by the point's
man. *Defensive rule:* Don't let the ball be dribbled between two
defensive men. Help recover.

If the ball is moved from G to G in the diagram and then
to the opposite wing area to the left, the movement would be as
shown in Diagram 178. Now the rules would be the same as
discussed with the ball on the right side. *Note:* Monster now
moves to back side as P moves to his side and responsibility.

The monster rules have covered the two-man front. If the

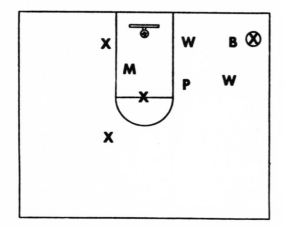

Diagram 176. Ball in Base area.

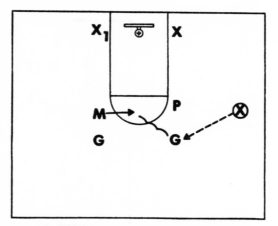

Diagram 177. Reversal pass 2-man front.

team gives the defense a one-man front, the point is on the ball and the monster free lances in the middle of the diamond or on his man. (See Diagram 179.) If the entry pass is made to the right, as in diagram 179, then the movement would be as shown. The base moves over, back wing maintains his relative distance, point drops between ball and basic spot, ball wing takes ball and monster falls off for his back-side responsibility.

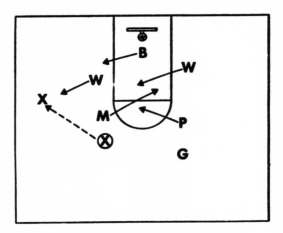

**Diagram 178. Shows movement to
Wing area from Monster side.**

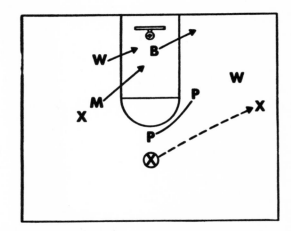

Diagram 179. Shows Monster 1-man front.

There will be times when the monster and point are pressing out in front and they do not get a chance to switch. As mentioned when traps are on, the wing and point should do the trapping. There may be times when the monster is on the pass when the entry pass is made to wing. The movement, then, will be just the same as shown in Diagram 178. This shift must be learned by the monster—his rule is to cover the back side.

Special coaching points for movement of the Wing when fronting low post: (See Diagram 180.) The wing's rule is to front the low post when the ball is in the corner. If a reversal pass is made, he must go over the top of the low post man, track 1. He should not go behind, track 2. In this way, he helps cut off any pass to the inside low. He must also try to help prevent a pass to any low post man on the opposite side of the lane.

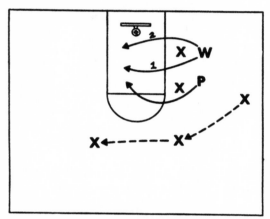

Diagram 180. Movement by W and P on reversal.

This same movement is also true for the point man as shown in Diagram 180. He must lead the high post man across and not follow him. These two men have to work hard in cutting the passing lanes into the middle. The base has to recover quickly from the corner but he needs help until he can recover from his pressure responsibility in the corner.

When the ball is brought down the court with the two-man front as shown in Diagram 181, the entry pass may, and can, be made to a high post man instead of to a wing. (See Diagram 181.) The movement now is for the base to come and the point to sag on this man. These two men try to squeeze this high post man. Both of the wings must drop quickly to front any low post men in base's area. Their movement is shown in Diagram 181. The monster now free-lances his movement until the ball is passed to a wing. He then will take back side and all movement and area responsibility will then be as discussed earlier.

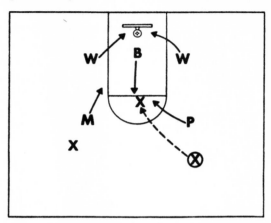

Diagram 181. Entry to high post.

The rebound triangle in the perimeter defense is always established by the positions of the men on the court. The perimeter long shooter is always boxed out for the long perimeter rebound. If a long shot is taken by a point man or a wing man, then it is their responsibility always to box this man while the other men work for position in their area. (See Diagram 182.)

Another advantage with the good rebounding coverage is the quick fast-break opportunities. Ball-side W's responsibility is to block for a long rebound and then he is in good position to release quickly down the side line. This same release is also there if the ball is shot from the corner and W does not secure the rebound. Now the release would be the same for the other wing if these shots were taken on the left side.

If the ball comes off away from the monster, then he also is in good position for a quick release on the opposite side from the wing. The point man's responsibility is first for the medium rebound and then release for the outlet pass. He almost always is in good position for the outlet pass.

If the ball is at the top of the key and is shot from that

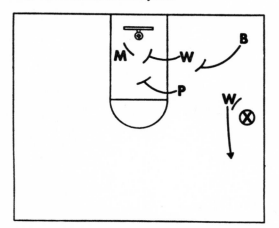

Diagram 182. Rebounding area shot by Wing; W—block, release.

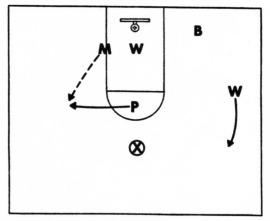

Diagram 183. Rebounding area shot top of key; W—block, release.

position, the men should be positioned as shown in Diagram 183. Now P blocks out a long rebounder. This puts M=W=B in good rebounding position. If the monster secures the rebound, the P can easily get to outlet zone, and out W can release quickly down the sideline.

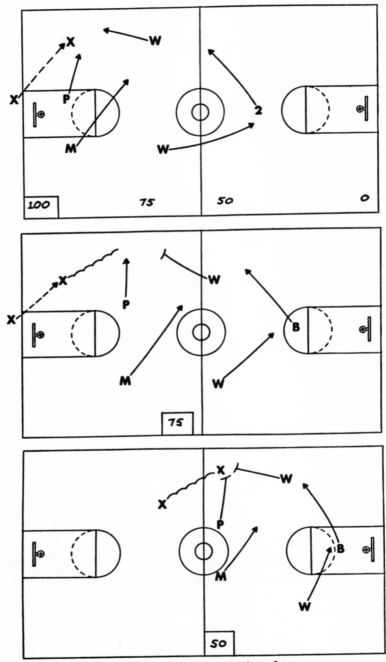

Diagram 184. Shows numbering of trap areas.

THE DIAMOND AND THE TRAP

The diamond and monster can be used and converted into a trap defense. The area of where the trap will be applied can be done easily by numbering the court as shown in Diagram 184.

The basic rules for our trap are:

1. Try to trap with point and wing.
2. The base is assigned to cover side where trap is being executed.
3. The Monster drops to cover middle.
4. The back side wing must cover passing lane to the basket.

When trapping at 75 or 100, the team is given the reversal pass. This pass does not break the trap situation. See Diagram 185 for movement on the reversal:

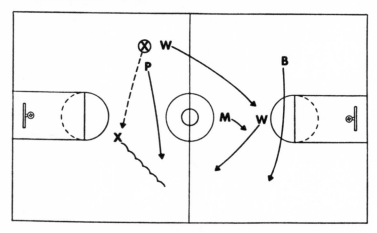

Diagram 185. Movement on reversal pass.

Now the wing comes up and pressures the man who received the reversal pass. If the man dribbles, the wing then tries to force him into point who comes across to continue to trap. Many teams feel once the reversal pass is made that the trap is broken. If good pressure is put on by the wing man, the team feels the ten-second count and at times then hurries the next pass. The monster now shuts off any pass into the middle, the base moves toward the basket and looks for the interception along the side line, and the opposite wing who was in the original trap must work hard to recover to shut off the passing lane to the basket. If the trap is broken at any time and the offense does not get the shot, the defensive team sets up in its called Monster Defense, pressure or perimeter.

When the point is pressuring the guard into the trap area, the offense man, at times, will try to reverse pivot to get himself into the middle of the court and to break away from the trapping wing. A special trapping situation then can be executed with the monster and the point. (See Diagram 186.) As the guard turns his back and starts the reversal, the monster tries to trap with the point. Now the two wings will try to cover the two outside passing lanes. The monster and point must not let the ball be passed into the middle—this is the really vulnerable area. The base in this trap protects the passing line to the basket. If the trap is broken, the team falls back into its perimeter zone defense.

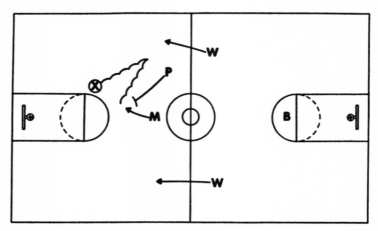

Diagram 186. Monster—Point trapping.

The success of the above trap depends on hard work by the point to make the man use his left hand and then trying to overplay so as to make the offense man reverse without the wing declaring himself to the trap. This is a good working trap between the point and monster.

A special alignment that is used occasionally with the 50 and 75 trap is shown in Diagram 187. When meeting and trying to pressure the ball, the monster and point have their backs to the side line as they try to channel the ball to the middle. They are responsible for the ball being passed in the middle or penetrating by a dribble between them. The two wings have their backs to the middle and try to cut off the long passing lane down the side. If the dribbler is forced to the side line, now the wing and point on that side trap, monster goes to the middle, base comes over, and opposite wing cuts off the passing lane to the basket. If the trap is broken, no shot develops and the team sets up, then the defense becomes the perimeter defense.

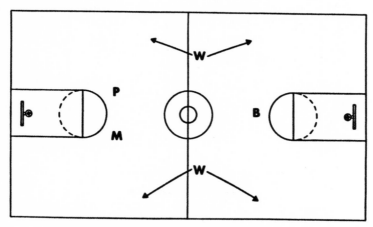

Diagram 187. Special 75 alignment.

To make trapping rules the same, the trap will usually be done by a wing and the point. The point and monster will push hard out in front as if in man-for-man. The monster will push hard and force his man to the middle to the point so he can shift off and force the dribbler into trap area. The monster may also overplay the middle and force to the side. The shift between monster and point will be as the wing comes up to trap. The point will just slide behind the monster and trap with the wing. The monster is now in the middle and protects his area. These two shifts have to be worked on by these two men. The point man will usually be the smaller guard so he can harass, while the monster is a bit bigger and hard to pass over in the trapping situations.

If from scouting reports a team has shown that they have a tendency to move the ball to the corner, the zero (0) trap can be used as shown in Diagram 188. This will be a special trap situation that is used along with the Basic Perimeter defense. *Note:* Point violates rule—stay between Basic X and ball. This area must be guarded by W.

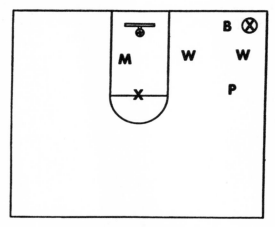

Diagram 188. Zero trap.

The team can use the various trap situations many different ways along with its man-for-man pressure defense. The coach may set up its regular 75 trap on baskets made, on free throws and side out-of-bounds use its 50 trap, and the rest of the time the team will be in its man-for-man defense. There may be times during the game when the defense will push hard full court man-for-man and try to disrupt the club and fall right into its perimeter defense. By always pushing full court, the defense disguises what defense is being used.

If a team wishes to push the defense harder in the

diamond, it can use the Diamond Pressure. If the Diamond Pressure is used, the areas each man has to cover are expanded. These areas of expansion are shown in Diagram 189. The rules are basically the same as in the perimeter but more and harder pressure is exerted. By putting on this pressure, it is trying to force the offense out higher on the court. Now this added pressure can create more openings but again it might force more turnovers. It does force the offense out higher on the court.

One trapping situation that becomes automatic is when the point and monster are pushing hard with the point on the ball. If the point gets beaten down the side line, that wing must come up and shut off the penetration and try to stop the dribbler. Man-for-man might be the defense but this forces us into our monster defense which can be either pressure or perimeter.

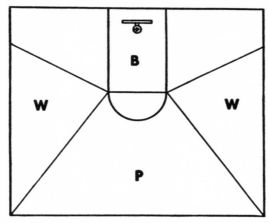

Diagram 189. Area for pressure.

Why the Diamond and the Monster:

1. A coach can hide and use the small man. By placing him at the point he is not going to be hurt by being taken inside.

2. With the movement of the personnel in the zone it continues to cut off passing lanes to the inside.

3. If the disguise of the traps by the diamond and monster are executed properly by good pressure out in front, it creates confusion in the offense as to what type of defense is being applied. If this confusion can force a few turnovers or get an offense to think other than to react, then it is serving the team's need.

4. The Diamond and Monster gives the team a good rebounding triangle. It has a man blocking out the long shooter.

5. It places men in good fast-break areas for outlet passes and releasing.

6. The defense can help the team control the tempo of the game. By trapping, it can help speed up the game or by dropping into its basic perimeter defense it can slow up the offense by clogging up the middle.

The Diamond and Monster, along with the denying man-for-man defense, can combine to make a variety of defensive situations for the coach to use in his defensive philosophy.

Zone Trap Offense   12

    A team will meet many types of full-court traps. There are numerous ways to attack them. Each ball club has to spend many hours in developing its confidence to attack the trap. The traps are designed to create turnovers and this is the one thing a team must work to prevent.

    The coach should have a set offense that, with a few adjustments, can meet these various types of traps. It is time consuming to try to teach a different type of offense for each different type of trap.

    An offense set that can be used to meet various types of traps is the 1-2-1-1 alignment as shown in Diagram 190.

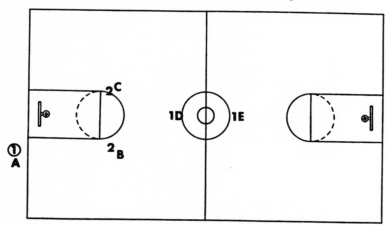

Diagram 190. Offensive Zone Trap Alignment.

The letters are used just for following through on the movements that will be discussed.

Player B breaks to receive the ball. Let's assume he receives the ball as shown in Diagram 191. B should receive the ball so that he can move it back and not too close to the baseline. B's first move is to turn and look up court—he should not use up the dribble. His passing options are to D who breaks to the side line, C breaking to the middle, or back to A.

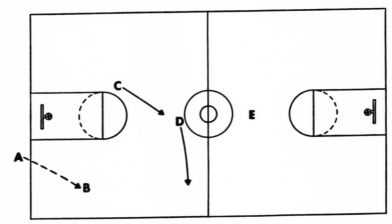

Diagram 191. Shows movement after inbounds pass.

A zone trapping offense should try to spread the defense and make the defense cover the entire court. What option is open to B depends on the trap and its alignment.

Option 1—hit D. If this option is hit, then D-E-C try to spread themselves and move the ball up the court. The offense tries to get a 3-on-2 advantage.

Option 2—hit C in the middle. Now C-D-E once again spread the defense and hope to get a 3-2 advantage.

If D is not hit when breaking to the side line, he continues his movement and breaks to the basket. This forces the defense to have at least the one man back.

Option 3—Hit A. A principle that should be adhered to is always have a man back to pass to if a trap is successful. Option 3 will be hit more often than either of the other two options, but option 2 is the main option. The players should now be approximately in position as shown in Diagram 192. A now tries to dribble up what could be a clear outside. As he is moving up, E breaks for the ball. If E can be hit, then E-C-D try to attack the basket.

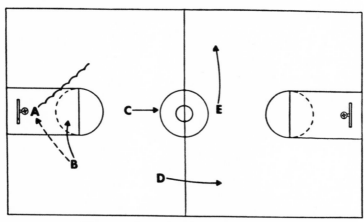

Diagram 192. Shows movement and position, ball moved to A.

If A can't hit E, then he tries to advance the ball up. B now is the back man in case A is trapped. Once a man is in the middle, like C, he tries also to free himself for a pass from A. Now the players are well spread and just try to free-lance the ball up the court.

If B is not open in Diagram 192, then A moves the ball to C. Now the movement and options are the same as when B was hit. (See Diagram 193.) Now C has the options of hitting D, B, or moving the ball back to A.

The third passing option for A is to hit D breaking up. B—broke,—can't be hit; C, broke and can't be hit; now D has to be the release man and get free. The men now are as shown in Diagram 194.

The reason B or C couldn't be hit is that they were overplayed, so the first passing option of D is to hit B or C. If this pass is open, then B-C-E try to advance the ball up the court.

If D can't make the breaking pass to B or C, then he moves the ball back to A. Now the court is spread defensively and offensively and the team tries to free-lance the ball up the court.

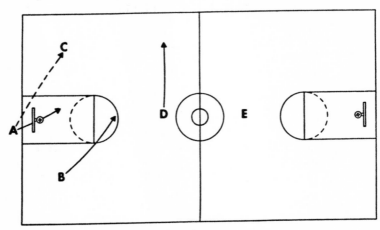

Diagram 193. Shows movement, inbounds pass to C.

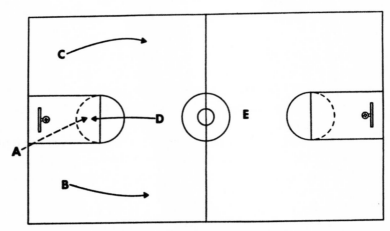

Diagram 194. Shows movement, inbounds pass to D.

In review, a few ideas that are important in any press offense:

1.   The players have to be ready to meet the press. This readiness has to be mental as well as physical. To get a team

ready mentally, a coach has to practice many times against the press so that the players will have confidence in beating it.

2. Keep the defense spread. The larger the area the team has to cover, the more work is demanded by the defense. Spreading out the defense will create openings for the offensive players as they try to advance the ball up the court.

3. , The players should have enough confidence in their ability to advance the basketball so that they want to attack the basket. I know that many times teams or players will be content just to break the press, but fail in their opportunity to try to score. This failure gives the defense even a greater opportunity to gamble on the press, if the team is just content to break it and not advance the ball to the basket.

INDEX

B

Back Track, 29
Ball handler, 144
Baseline Pick for Corner, 105-106
Baseline Pick for Post, 103-105
Baseline Track, 29-32
Basic Working Formation:
    back to original strong side, 43-46
    Back Track, 29
    basic pattern from each series the
        same, 55
    Baseline Track, 29-32
    baskets made, 55
    continuity when No. 5 man
        doesn't hit anyone,
        double screen, 37-42
    Double Screen, 49-52
    drive by WSW (No. 5), 35-37
    drive or shoot, 48-49
    free throws made or missed by
        other team, 55
    Front Track, 28
    hit cutter (2 man), 27-28
    hit No. 1 man in corner, 20-22
    hit No. 3 man (post), 32-35
    hit No. 4 man, 24-27
    hit post, No. 3 man, 22-24
    hit the post, 46-48
    maneuverability, 55
    reasons for different series, 55
    reset, 52
    reset by WSW, 42-43
    Strong-Side Split, 22
    Ten Series Entry Strong Side, 55-64
        (see also Ten Series Entry
        Strong Side)
    Ten Series Entry Weak Side, 64-68
    Thirty Series, 19, 71-73
        (see also Thirty series)
    time for series to be run, 55
    Twenty Series, 19, 69-71
        (see also Twenty Series)

use of all three series, 55
Weak-Side Split, 33
Zone offense, 112
Baskets made, 91
BC, 105
"Blind pig":
    1-4 formation, 179
    Overhead to the Post, 103
    V cut, 79
Blocking game, 169

C

"C," 92
Control game, 136
Cutter:
    delayed offense, 131
    rebounder, 126
    sets opposite post, 124-126

D

Delayed offense:
    hit SSW, 131-136
    hit WSW, 131
    options of cutter, 131
    review control game, 136
    WSW options, 129-131
        acceptable shots, 129
        ball to cutter breaking out, 131
        BWF, 129
        double-screen situation, 129-130
        drive, 129
        no out shots, 129
        post is hit, 129
        reset, 129
        shooting, 129
        SSW, 130, 131
Denial defenses:
    alertness and reaction, 167
    ball not dribbled between defensive
        player and baseline, 159
    ball not dribbled between two
        defensive players, 158-160

Denial defenses: *(Cont.)*
    diamond and monster, 189
    fast break, 164-166
    force the bad pass, 167
    line of flight, 161-162
    playing dribbler, 167
    post, 162-163
        high, 162
        low, 162
        medium, 162-163
    review, 168-169
    screen, 163-164
    shuffle, 166-167 *(see also*
        Shuffle)
    strongly right-handed offensive, 167
    traps, 169-175 *(see also* Traps)
    when dribbler picks up dribble, 167
Diamond and monster:
    areas of responsibility, 189
    base, 190
    basic perimeter defense, 189, 190-198
        (see also Perimeter-diamond-
        monster defense)
    biggest guard or best defensive
        "head," 190
    confusion as to type of defense, 204
    denying principles, 189
    good rebounding triangle, 204
    hide and use small man, 203
    monster, 190
    passing lanes to inside cut off, 203
    personnel placement, 189-190
    point, 189
    post man and biggest forward,
        189-190
    quickest and smallest forward, 190
    smallest guard, 189
    tempo, 204
    trap, 199-203
        automatic situation, 203
        basic rules, 199
        Diamond Pressure, 203
        50 and 75, 201
        making rules the same, 201
        point pressuring guard, 200
        reversal pass, 199
        75 or 100, 199
        use many different ways, 202
        where applied, 199
        zero (0), 202
    variety of defensive situations, 204
    why, 203-204
    wings, 189-190
Double-Screen:
    shots, 137
    SSW, 49-52
    Zone offense, 118-120

Double-Screen Shooting Drill, 150-151
Dribble, 18
Drills:
    Double-Screen Shooting, 150-151
    Lay-Up and Dribbling, 152-153
    One-On-One Defensive, Full
        Court, 155
    Scramble, 147-150
    3-On-2 Fast-Break, 153-154
    3-On-3, Full Court, 154-155
    Weak-Side-Wing Shooting, 151-152
Drive, 48-49
Driver, 144

E

"11C," 92
"11CI," 98
"11CR," 99

F

Fast break:
    denial defense, 164-166
    diamond and monster, 196
50 trap, 201, 202
Formations, 16-18
Forward, 144
Fouling, 170
Free-lancing, 143
Free throw made, 91
Front Track, 28-29

G

Guard, 143, 144, 145
Guard on to the post, 86-88
Guard underneath, 81-82

H

High post area, denial defense, 162
Highest post position, 137

I

"I," 93,98
Interchange and Clear, 98
Interchanging:
    "blind pig," 79
    drive to outside, post as screen, 79
    guards underneath, 81-82
    hit 4 breaking, 79
    hit SSF coming around, 79
    keeps pattern moving, 82
    options, 79
    run any guard on to weak side, 82
    teaches movement without ball, 82
    V cut, 77-81

K

Keys, 18

L

Lay-Up and Dribbling Drill, 152-153
Letter, call out, 92
Line of flight, 161
Low post area, denial defense, 162
Low post position, 137

M

Medium post area, denial defense,
  162-163
Movements:
  back to original strong side, 43-46
  back track, 29
  ball down weak side, 137
  baseline track, 29-32
  Basic Working Formation, 18-54
  defense dictates pass open, 141
  double screen, 37-42
      49-52
  dribble, 18
  drive by WSW (No. 5), 35-37
  drive or shoot, 48-49
  formations, 16-18
  front track, 28
  high post position, 137
  hit center, 141
  hit cutter (2 man), 27-28
  hit No. 1 man in corner, 20-22, 142
  hit No. 4 man, 24-27, 32-35
  hit post, 22-24, 46-48
  hit strong-side forward, 141
  hit weak-side guard, 141
  key, 18
  look at post, 142
  low post position, 137
  numbering of personnel, 17
  pass, 18
  player who has ball, 18
  reset by SSW, 52
  reset by WSW, 42-43
  reverse floor to No. 4 man, 142
  rotate, 142
  sagging defense, 138
  sequence of options, 141
  Tandem Left, 16, 17, 141-142
  Tandem Right, 16, 17
  team pressuring No. 2, 139
  weak-side forward, 142
  weak-side guard, 142
  when No. 5 doesn't hit anyone,
      37-42

N

Number, call out, 91, 92
Numbering, personnel, 17

O

1-4 formation and shuffle:
  advantage, 178
  "blind pig," 179
  BWF established before shuffle
      movement started, 178
  center, 180-181
  double-screen situation, 181
  height of positions, 177-178
  instead of Tandem formations, 177
  instead of two-man front, 177
  LW options, 179-180
  no shots develop, 179
  No. 2 man options, 179
  numbers and men, 177
  point man hits RP, 178
  point passing to wing, 181
  point starts movement at right wing,
      178
  positions each player runs, 177
  post pops to point position, 181
  RW hit, 178, 179
  special situations, 184-186
  strong-side wing, 180
  Ten and Twenty Series, 178
  Twenty Series, 180
  two good post men, 181
  use of personnel, 180-184
  use on entering BWF, 177
  well-executed pass by point, 178
  zone, 186-188
100 trap, 199
One-On-One Defensive Drill, Full
  Court, 155
1-2-1-1, 170, 205
OP, 100
Out of bounds, 91
Overhead to Post:
  basic movement, 101
  Basic Working Formation, 101, 103
  "blind pig," 103
  cutter, 101
  defensive man on post, 101
  from any of three series, 99
  from either formation, 99
  pass did not work, 101, 102
  SSW, 103
  "21OP," 99
  when certain play called, 101
  WSF, 103
  WSW, 103
Overloads, 111

P

Pass, 18
Passer, 145
Pattern ball club, 169
Perimeter-diamond-monster defense:
    ball at top of key, 196-197
    ball comes off away from monster,
        196
    base, 190
    like man for man defense, 191
    M=W=B, 197
    monster, 191
    monster rules, 192
    one-man front, 193
    point, 190
    push ball by point man, 192
    quick fast-break opportunities, 196
    reason, 190
    rebound triangle, 196
    release, 196
    rule for point-wings-base, 190-191
    trapping, 194
    two-man front, 192
    wing-back side, 190
    wing-ball side, 190
    wing fronting low post, 195
Placement players:
    ball handler, 144
    diamond and monster, 189-190
    different types of players, 143
    driver, 144
    forward, 144
    guard, 143, 144, 145
    higher post, 137
    low post, 137
    1-4 and shuffle, 180-184
    passer, 145
    player able to run each position,
        142, 143
    post position, 144
    reason for different series, 55
    shooter, 144
    strength and weaknesses, 137
    weak-side forward, 142
    weak-side guard, 142
    Zone, 121-123
Player who has ball, 18
Plays, special, 91-109
    (*see also* Special plays)
Point, hit, 113
Post:
    cutter sets opposite, 124-126
    denial defense, 162-163
    hit, 113
    position, 137, 144

R

Reset:
    SSW, 52
    WSW, 42-43
Reversal pass, 199
Rotation:
    ball back to forward, 83
    ball to corner, 83
    BWF, 83
    forward becomes 5 man, 83
    guard into the post, 86-88
    hit No. 2 man, 85-86
    moving screen for post, 83
    rotate center off post, 83
    weak side forward rotates to post, 83
Rotation and Clear, 99

S

Sagging defense, 138
Scramble Drill:
    Basic Working Formation, 147
    beginning of year, 150
    defensive man added, 149
    diagram, 137
    drilling dummy, 149
    final step of full court, 149
    half-court controlled, 149
    hardest part of teaching, 149
    limited defense, 149
    post end basket, 148
    reviewing fundamentals already
        taught, 148
    teaching certain option, 148
    weak phase of pattern, 150
Screen, denial defense, 163-164
Series, basic, 15-54 (*see also* Basic Work-
    ing Formation)
75 trap, 199, 201, 202
Shoot or drive, 48-49
Shooter, 144
Shuffle:
    denial, 166-167
        overplaying of point man, 167
        pass to Shuffle Cutter, 166
        pass to weak-side wing, 166
        pressure weak-side forward and
            sag, 167
    1-4 formation and shuffle, 177-188
        (*see also* 1-4 formation and
            shuffle)
    players must get to certain spots, 166
    very controlled, 166
Slow-up game (*see* Delayed offense)

Special plays:
  Baseline Pick for Corner, 105-106
  Baseline Pick for Post, 103-105
  calling out, 91
  different personnel in different
    spots, 93
  examples of situations and plays, 92
  foul, 91
  Interchange and Clear, 98
  number and letter called, 92
  1-4 formation, 184-186
  Overhead to Post, 99-103
    (*see also* Overhead to Post)
  play to be run, 92
  resemble basic pattern, 91
  review, 106-107
  Rotation and Clear, 99
  run play many ways, 93
  series to be run, 92
  special clear out from pattern,
    107-109
  start from BWF, 91
  Strong Side Clear, 93-98
    (*see also* Strong Side Clear)
  Tandem Left, No. 2 formation, 92
  Tandem Right, No. 1 formation, 92
  weak defensive man, 93
  when doesn't work, 91
Strengths, 137
Strong Side Clear:
  free throw shot by opponents, 93
  if none of clear options works, 96-97
  lay-up or jump shot, 94
  No. 1 formation, Tandem Right
    Formation, 92, 93
  one of most successful, 93
  other option to run, 93
  overplaying and freelance, 93
  reset, into pattern to left side, 97, 98
  reset, run to clear other side, 97-98
  revert to original pattern, 93
  starting, 93
  when No. 4 man starts drive to right,
    94
Strong-Side split, 22
Strong Side, zone offense, 123-124

                    T

Tandem Left, 16, 17, 112, 141-142
Tandem Right, 16, 112
Tempo, 169
Ten Series:
  first option of No. 1 man, 57-59
  review, Strong Side, 64
  second option of No. 1 man, 59

Ten Series: (*Cont.*)
  split to post from SSF, 70
  third option of No. 1 man, 60-63
Ten Series Entry Strong Side:
  big man as No. 3 man, 56
  clear out method, 56
  designating players to specific spots,
    56
  enter in strong side or weak side, 56
  guard without ball, 56, 57
  No. 1 man, 57-63
    hit No. 2 man, 57
    hit No. 3 man, 59
    hit No. 4 man, 60-63
  pressured full court, 56
  review, 64
  starting basic pattern, 55-64
  Tandem Right or Tandem Left, 56
  teaching to start pattern, 56
  weak side or strong side, 56
  where pressure applied, 56
Ten Series Entry Weak Side:
  bring the ball up weak side, 65-68
  Left Side in Basic Working Formation,
    65
  movement of No. 5 man, 67-68
  options, 67
  pattern of play, 65
  pressure of defense on 1, 65
  shoot in front of post, 67
Thirty Series:
  hit corner; rotate or split, 73
  hit post and split, 73
  moving screen for 5 man, 71
  options available to No. 2, 73
  reverse floor to point, 73
  run from No. 1 and No. 2 formations, 71
  zone offense, 112
3-On-2 Fast-Break Drill, 153-154
3-On-3 Drill, Full Court, 154-155
Time, 111
Traps:
  ball away from medium and high post,
    175
  ball not dribbled between two
    defensive players, 171
  ball out of percentage area, 175
  blocking game, 169
  combination, 169
  defensive man moves when ball
    moves, 175
  diamond and monster, 199-203
    (*see also* Diamond and
      monster)
  disguised, 175

Traps: *(Cont.)*
  50, 201, 202
  fouling, 170
  front low post, 175
  full-court, 169
  half-court, 169
  keep offensive team guessing, 175
  match-up zones, 169
  100, 199
  1-2-1-1, 170
  pattern ball club, 169
  players assume number and
      assignments, 173
  practice, 175
  pressure on man with ball, 175
  rules for movement and area,
      171, 172
  75, 199, 201, 202
  tempo of game, 169
  zero, 202
  zone trap offense, 205-209
Trouble spots:
  interchanging, 75-82
      (see also Interchanging)
  review, 88-89
  rotation, 83-88 *(see also* Rotation)
"12CI," 92
"21BC," 105
"21BP," 103
"21OP," 99
Twenty Series:
  baskets made, 55
  free throws made or missed by
      other team, 55
  guard and forward positions, 69
  hit center and split, 69
  hit 2 man in corner, 69
  hit 4 man; 1 becomes cutter, 69
  1-4 and shuffle, 180
  options for No. 2, 69
  split to post from SSF, 70
  status of No. 2 man, 70
  Tandem Formations, 69
  zone offense, 112
"22C," 93

V

V cut, 77-81

W

Weaknesses, 137
Weak-side forward, 142
Weak-side guard, 142
Weak-Side Split, 33
Weak-Side Wing:
  delay offense, 129-131
  zone offense, 115-118
Weak-Side-Wing Shooting Drill, 151-152

Z

Zero trap, 202
Zone offense:
  back to original strong Side, 123-124
  ball, movement, 111
  basic movement same for each
      defense, 127
  Basic Working Formation, 112
  cutter rebounder, 126
  cutter sets opposite post, 124-126
  double-screen movement, 126
  man, movement, 111
  many types of zones encountered,
      111
  1-4 formation, 186-188
  overloads, 111
  personnel, placement, 121-123
  pressure vary, 113
  review, 126-127
  same as for man-to-man, 111
  SSF with ball in BWF, 113-115
    hit the corner, 113
    hit the point, 113-115
    hit the post, 113
  Tandem Right and Tandem Left, 112
  teams change defenses, 126
  Ten, Twenty, and Thirty Series, 112
  terminology, 126
  time, 111, 112, 126
  two basic movements, 111
  type of movement, 126
  use of different series and movement,
      113
  Weak Side Wing, 115-118
    cutter, 115
    double screen, 118-120
    post is hit, 117
    reset, 118
  where shots develop, 126
Zone trap offense, 205-209